Rebirth II

By:
Jonathan

Rebirth II
Book Five of the Series *The Nine*
May 22, 2018, *First Edition*

Copyright © 2018

Cover Photo Credit: Brandon Wong

All rights reserved. This book or any portion thereof may not be reproduced or used in any manner whatsoever without the express written permission of the publisher except for the use of brief quotations in a book review or scholarly journal.

ISBN-13: 978-1-942967-33-0

KreativeMinds Publishing
www.kreativeminds.net

Ordering Information:

Special discounts are available on quantity purchases by corporations, associations, educators, and others. For details, contact the publisher at the above listed address or the email address below.

U.S. trade bookstores and wholesalers: Please use the email address below. email: publishing@kreativeminds.net

To My King, through whom all things are possible.

Always,
Jonathan

Introduction

This is the second book of my journals, the words of the experiences shown to me by God. Book V – Rebirth II covers a period of time from December 25, 2013 through March 24, 2014. These are the days God spoke to me more than ever before. These are the days that God called upon me to take a leap of faith in His words. I believe there has to be a point in everyone's life when their soul is tested more than they thought they could endure. For me, that test came in a way that may not seem like a breaking point to others. But, to me, this test was a moment that I pleaded to God to stop if it was going to set me up for heartbreak. It was my breaking point. It was the point I knew I would lose the framework of my life that I had struggled to rebuild. Every piece of my soul was once shattered into a million pieces upon the floor, but had been carefully rebuilt by hand over years of pain. This fragility was placed into the trust of God's hands. In the end, I had to fall. I had to fail. I had to feel Him catch me when I thought I would surely hit the ground. This was the moment I understood unbridled trust and felt the removal of all fear. This was my story's equivalent moment to Abraham's test with Isaac. This was the moment I truly understood His strength and Love as I demonstrated my faith in Him.

Always,
Jonathan

Wonders (Part 2)

The days leading into the darkness of my life were the first steps I took forward into His grand light. And though I would not initially see the light in the beginning, I did manage to sense a primal tugging at the depths of my soul encouraging me to seek out its source. The recognition of this tugging would appear through a veil to earthly eyes as a curiosity, an intrigue, an itch – possibly even a cry out for help. Even as it first appeared to me, I sought rationalization to the changes happening in my life through science, academics, and reason. I never let go of faith for I always understood it to be the source, the truth. But I wanted to see faith through the eyes of reason in order to add clarity to the gray. And so it would be, this is how the journey began and how God helped me begin to learn how to see.

As it was revealed in Part 1 of Wonders in Book IV – Rebirth I, the life I once knew held within it a greater mystery than I was capable of seeing without a forced change-of-perspective. During the first portion of the journey, God would use the questions I was asking Him to help me learn to communicate and hear His Voice. By the end of Book IV – Rebirth I, three things were certain. The first certainty was that through humbling myself as a child and asking Him to

Rebirth II

teach me as a child would learn – with no preconceived notions – I was learning how to hear His Voice.

The second certainty was that all it took was a question – one single question on the evening of November 25, 2011 – and God would answer. And isn't that amazing? One. Just one. That is all it took for God to respond. November 25, 2011, was the very first day God would begin speaking to me in the most spectacular way. Or perhaps, maybe it is best said that November 25, 2011, was the very first day I acknowledged to Him that I was completely ready to truly listen – with no preconceived notions or expectations on how He would answer. And while I would not see it that way at first since I was a child just learning how to listen, learning how to see, this date would be seen as another marker on His Divine timeline, similar to the marker of my baptism on December 24, 1989 – a date discussed in Wonders, Part 1. These dates are important. This is the second certainty.

The third certainty was that through the demonstration of the continued dedication of learning to hear His Voice, He helped strengthen my soul, which in turn allowed me to be open to the receipt of Divine communication when His Will implored. Jesus once preached about humbling oneself as a child. To many modern day believers, the most accepted translation of this preaching is for the soul to be curious, to have a wonder about Him. Even as I learned to see as a child, I could not express in words what it truly means to humble oneself as a child. It takes a moment of splendid grace and humility to understand we are only vessels, lenses of our Crea-

Wonders (Part 2)

tor, an infinitely micro understanding of an infinitely macro Love. To see God through the eyes of a child while carrying the respect of an adult is a portion of the meaning, but the full meaning is for each soul to explore. It may be uncomfortable and difficult, but that feeling is just ego holding on…a feeling every person is far too scared to admit exists. However, it is a feeling like the weight of the world falling away once a soul demonstrates the strength to allow it to subside.

By the end of Book IV – Rebirth I, I had grown from an academically (and ego-driven) embodiment of a soul into a humble child with eyes of wonder, willfully laying down ego in lieu of humble gratitude of His Grand Divine. I had returned to how I once arrived on this Earth. It was through this childlike wonder that the journey was allowed to take the form that it has. And, most certainly, the journey can always change course. But through the motion and momentum of a child learning to see, learning to speak, learning to walk, and eventually learning to run, the journey moves forward in ways unimaginable and unfathomable to mankind's point of view.

The ending of Book IV brought about an understanding of a calling, though I was yet unsure what it would mean. In truth, it is possible that this writing is as it was always intended to be. It was just left upon my soul to find the recognition and learn how to see. I cannot help but think that the story unfolding through God's lessons is like reading a history of one's own life as it was and before it is. There is an undeniable curiosity about the concept of freewill and predestination, but why can it not be both? What if we are all capable of becoming Kings

Rebirth II

even though few will ever desire to question or seek out the path? At first it may seem irreverent to even discuss the possibility of the idea of becoming more than man. But the more I have come to understand the Lord's words, the more I have come to understand that becoming more than man is the purpose. In becoming more than man, the soul is actually shedding the form of clay and revealing the source of All That Is. It is not the man that is the light, or even the performer of miracles, but rather the faith in the Lord shining through the vessel's doorway in order to perform an action of Divine magnitude in the name of Love.

And if it is seen that this possibility can be granted to all that seek Him, then it should also be understood that the vessel also has the potential to be a doorway for darkness. With greater understanding comes greater responsibility. It should be clear that the Words written are intended to be held with the greatest respect for our Father. A man can use a hammer to build a house or use that very same hammer for destruction. His Words are in the same vein. For nearly every religion and every divide have chosen to use His Words – regardless of written source – as a tool of separation rather than of unity and light. Somehow, those who have preached the loudest have missed the most important theme. We are all One, brothers and sisters in Christ, serving Him and preparing the world for the return of the Messiah.

As it would begin to be revealed to me along this journey, the road to the Kingdom would lead me through a series of leaps of faith – the final being the biggest leap of all. One of

Wonders (Part 2)

the first leaps is brought to light in this book through God asking me to blindly follow His commands in a place where I was most vulnerable. To some, this portion of the journey will be seen as the hopeful longing to be with someone I held dear. But it should be understood that this was the leap. These were the moments that I was learning to hear His voice through the world around me, through others, and directly through intimate conversations with Him.

Everyone has a choice. These were the days that I chose to follow His Voice all the while hoping that I would not shatter into a million pieces, which would be irrecoverable if the destination did not end with the desired results. These were the days that would shape me and demonstrate my walk of faith for my Father. This would be a time of tests and trials. There would be moments of splendor in literally hearing the Voice of God. But, there would also be moments of standing face-to-face with the devil quite literally. And though many will see this part of the journey through the lens of earthly eyes, it is important to see it for so much more.

In the beginning, the journey began as a coming of age ceremony – the year of thirty – but one I would not see until much later along the journey. It is a year symbolic to the life and times of Christ on Earth...as is the year of thirty-three, which is the time period during which this chapter's writing is taking place and the Books of Nine are taking their final form. While it won't be revealed until the continuation of Wonders in Books VI and VII, the markers corresponding to the experiences of my life that were placed upon His Divine timeline, are of utmost importance to understand. These markers are possibly the most important signals God has provided for the reader to understand the source of these words.

These words were not created, but rather brought into existence through the experiences I have been blessed to be. And through the humble walk of becoming, the Lord has spoken through this embodiment according to such a divine timeline in order to bring further significance to the message He has tasked me to share – the message forthcoming. So as this portion of the journey is read, it should be observed as tests, trials, and learning to understand the manner in which the Lord asked me to believe.

These were the times He wanted to see hope through me, wanted to see desire, wanted to see the passion inside of me unfolding in a way wherein I would place the complete embodiment of the rush of emotions in the hands of His protection. The words in this book are the light of understanding as to how the Books of Nine would one day come to be. At first I thought the Lord was just helping me see the form of the first book, the story of Gravity Calling. But as His words took shape, it became apparent that His plan was much greater than just a story. It was a plan to share His story of Ever-After, preceding the return of His Almighty Glory. And though that message will be revealed more in depth in the continuation of Wonders to come, this book is His continued revelation of a child learning to see.

The Written (cont'd)

"The Written" is the continued portion of the journey from when I recognized I was standing in the desert of my personal version of Leviticus through a moment I can only describe as a free-fall-leap-of-faith into the hands of my Father. This is a time when the words spoken to me were much more intimate and pregnant with meaning than ever before.

Rebirth II is a time period that reflects a much clearer understanding of where God had been leading and how he led me to hear His voice. In the beginning, I relied on science as my guide. By the end of Rebirth I, the journey had become more spiritual than I had ever imagined. In this book, many of the experiences center on the Love interest in my life and the lessons God intended for me to learn through Love. This was a time that God steered me through a jungle of fear as I learned to hear His voice through the trees, guiding me home. And while I elaborate on the meaning of it all in Book II – Crowns, the important takeaway through this book is that I leapt, and He caught me with open arms.

I never could have imagined how God could have become so intimate during this part of the journey with me. It was as if there was only His voice guiding every emotion and attempt at rationalization through the process. This is a portion of time

Rebirth II

where I still did not write down all of my earthly experiences, though He was working just as hard in my life in those unwritten times as well. Perhaps I was afraid that if I journaled how I thought I was being tested in my daily walk that it would make me look crazy. I was not sure how much I needed to journal about my trials and tribulations. But what I eventually did learn during those times, was that He was speaking to me daily, in every way imaginable. It was just up to me to begin listening for His voice.

So, while some of the entries in this book may seem like they reference something possibly missed in reading, the truth is that these entries were mostly intended to be a continuation of my visions and travels to heaven. But, as time progressed, I began seeing a need to write down more information about how the interactions in life came to pass. If I had planned from the beginning that all of these words would one day be put into book form, I probably would have approached it a little differently. It was not until the end of 2013 that everything started to fall into view. And, even then, it took partway through 2014 for me to realize the daily interactions were just as important to document. In July of 2014, I used my move to Fort Lauderdale as a transition point for that documentation. But even then, some of it was written in a different form for Book III – Kingdom. The first three books comprise His story. Books IV – VII are the journals from these times. And that is the most important aspect to remember about all of the words written.

...

The Written (cont'd)

December 25, 2013

I was in a city on the top of a great mountain. It was dark. Nightfall had overtaken the city. I walked into a restaurant that seemed extremely familiar. I was carrying something important in a box that was to be delivered upstairs. As I walked through the location, people were bustling about. When I reached the stairway there were two guards standing watch over the door. I explained I was supposed to take the box upstairs and they allowed me to pass.

When I reached the top, I entered a door and it opened into a beautiful room. This room only had a small couch and a chair along the wall – everything else was left open. I felt that I was standing in the presence of someone important (hence the guards), though I could not discern who it was at first. I noticed that the room was filled with people surrounding a girl – whom I identified as a holy presence. When the people turned and saw me enter the room, they all dispersed at her command. She saw me, and welcomed me in.

I placed the box on the couch, and she began to talk to me. I took off my jacket and sat it on the couch alongside the box. She was kind and welcoming – beautiful and svelte. She was tall and had long, flowing, sandy-blonde hair. I could tell she enjoyed my company, though I was nervous I would overstay my welcome. I cordially chatted with her and decided it was best to walk back down the stairs so as not to ruin my opportunity to see her again.

Rebirth II

As I reached the bottom of the stairs and began to head to the door, I realized I had left my jacket upstairs. I turned and headed back up. This time the guards were not present and I was freely able to pass back up the stairs. When I reached the top, I noticed the room was still empty. She was with a man in a narrow, offset room. He was helping her fix her hair. She was on her knees and he stood behind her. I did not see any mirrors in the room.

She began to talk to me again. I could tell she was glad I had returned. I told her I had left my jacket, and that I was sorry to intrude. She invited me into the room she was in as the guy left. The room was a bold, deep green. Along the walls I noticed gold inlays of various shapes. My eyes fell onto a word that was carved into the wall. The word was "chit." I ran my finger over it. The word was definitely carved into the wall, but etched in gold – as if the wall was made of gold, with green paint covering the shine.

Though I did not ask what the word was or meant, after the vision ended I researched the word and determined it was another Sanskrit word bestowed to me. This word means "true consciousness." It is part of the Brahman experience of Satchidānanda (being, consciousness, bliss). So as I stood before the girl, she continued to attempt to warm me up to a more in-depth conversation. I felt a tremendous amount of Love and attraction to her, which made me nervous about overstaying again. She mentioned something about a person named Jake. In reflection of the moment, I believe it was her nickname for a man named Jacob – possibly even calling out

The Written (cont'd)

my name to me. But when I first heard it, I responded, "Oh yeah, I had friends that knew him when you two were together, but I never attempted to cross-over to meet you." She gave me an odd look, as if I had not understood who she was talking about.

Honestly, I was not sure I knew what I was talking about – though my spirit was led to say those words. My fear of the situation unraveling kicked in, and I asked her if she would be around all night. She laughed and said that she would. She told me that I should come back. I looked at her somewhat puzzled as to how I would be able to get past the guards again. She smiled and said, "Just let Obeeda (or possibly Obdeia – I had a hard time repeating the name back to her when I tried to acknowledge I understood) know I would return. I said I would. We said our goodbyes. I walked out of the room unsure of who this person was that I should speak to.

There was a black woman with short silver hair sitting on the couch with a child. I asked her if she was Obeeda. She did not seem to understand the words, but shook her head slightly to indicate she was not the right person. I walked down the stairs. I stood next to a table, and many of the beings I identified as workers (though I am sure they were angels) came up and asked if I was okay or needed help. I asked them where I could find Obeeda but no one knew the name. I wandered around through the room and could not find anyone by that name and eventually stepped out of the building and into the street. It was dark and misty. I began to walk down a cobblestone path that headed down the mountain. I awoke.

Rebirth II

I journaled the previous vision, and afterwards, decided to go back to sleep even though the sun was starting to rise. As soon as I closed my eyes, I was standing at the base of a tall, slender mountain with a tall, winding staircase that reached up to the city above (though the view was obfuscated by the clouds). It was the mountain from my previous vision and my spirit had apparently continued to walk down the mountainside while my earthly body journaled the previous words. I was now standing in a small group of people that I had seen earlier in the night, all led by an oriental man. He was clearly our guide into and out from the city.

It was the first time I recall seeing this particular man. He was telling everyone that it was time to go – that he did not want anyone to overheat. He was escorting everyone down the stairs toward another gate to the mountain. Everyone appeared as zombies – no reactions, no life. I understood them to be unawakened spirits. I was a few paces behind the group, but when I caught up with them, I told the man that I was "really good and completely aware of where I was." I told him that I had questions, and I would be able to remember the answers. He smiled and said, "Okay." Though he looked unamused, he was intrigued enough to send everyone through the gates and take me partially back up the stairs to a plateau on the side of the mountain.

I asked if he was Obeeda and explained that I was told I could return. He smiled and said he was not. I felt that I was not in the right place to ask for Obeeda. As I turned to face the man more directly, he asked how I was feeling and if I was

The Written (cont'd)

overheating. I said, "I'm fine, but my coat feels like a marshmallow around my body and my face." I felt a puffy sensation along my cheeks. My body felt slightly encumbered from the coat I was wearing. In retrospect, I think the coat was the sensation of my pillow and comforter pushing against the face of my earthly body in bed. I thought about taking the coat off, but realized it would be too difficult with maintaining awareness, so I decided to continue the conversation.

I looked at him and said, "So, can you tell me what this is – where we are? I know this is not Earth. Is this technically part of Heaven? Is it a parallel dimension? Is it another world?" He smiled. He was amused. I told him I would remember – that I was aware. He responded, "Kind of. It's not really though. It is no man's land." My mind raced with questions. Was he indicating this was a spiritual dimension only? Was he indicating this was a place between Heaven and Earth? Was this an entry and exit point to the heavens? I could tell that the activity in my mind was causing me to lose harmony with the location I was in. I knew I had very little time left. I began to ask another question. As I began to speak, the air felt like it was being sucked out of me. He smiled (obviously aware this would happen the longer we spoke) and asked if I was okay – though I could tell he already knew the answer. I could not catch my breath well enough to form an answer. He held up a Polaroid camera and asked me to smile. As I did, the bulb flashed in a great burst of light and I returned to Earth to write about the experience.

Rebirth II

December 25, 2013
7:00 p.m.

For a brief moment during meditation, I was running with a group of others down a sidewalk. We were within a gated area, but the middle area (to my left) had a great expanse of a park. There were buildings all around. It seemed like a college campus with lush foliage and well-manicured grass. As I ran, I pulled away in front of the others in the group. In my left hand held between my thumb and forefinger was a metallic disk. It was made of bronze or iron and had a bronze hue. It was important to hold it out with my arm extended from my body. In reference to my size, the disc had a diameter of approximately two and a half inches and a thickness of one and a half inches. Whatever the situation was, I was entertained. I felt like I was winning at some game and sort of invincible in a childlike way. Suddenly from behind I heard a young male's voice shout out, "Protect the lady of the lake as the devil will come through." My mind began to race with thoughts causing me to fall out of harmony with the location and return to Earth.

December 27, 2013

Last night I had several heavenly experiences though I was unable to bring them back with me to write about. I had trouble regulating my body to remain in harmony with the location. Each time I awoke, all I could recall was being told to

The Written (cont'd)

"regulate." This is a word I rarely – if ever – use in my daily routine. But I recall I was told over and over again to "regulate" – no doubt due to my inability to maintain harmony with the moment. It was also important that I remembered to adhere to the "speed limit" which I understood to mean how quickly I can advance in spiritual growth to maintain an optimal balance of that which I can bring back to Earth. It would seem the faster I try to learn, the harder it is for me to bring any information back with me. And this would have been true about last night's experiences because I prepared a laundry list of items I wanted to discuss as I readied my body to visit the heavens.

I can recall that I discussed Aaron's rod from the Bible. I can recall that one of the stones of his staff that begins with the letter A was actually a different stone than has been popularly translated, but again, I was unable to bring back the information with me this time. I was also imparted knowledge about a stone – Alexandrite. This information was significant to retain, as it has importance in my life at this time. I am unsure of how this relates to anything yet (since I have not spent any time working or even trying to understand crystals, rocks, or minerals) but I do plan to research the stone and learn about its properties and why I may have been imparted this information.

Rebirth II

December 27, 2013
3:00 p.m.

As I sat down to pray, I felt the spirit move within my body. As I prayed, I realized that my prayer was not just a question, but was a dialogue. My Lord heard my cry and so He began to converse. The spirit began to swirl inside of my body. From the seat of my spine through my crown I felt a counterclockwise vortex of energy ignited my very being. The vortex felt like a double helix of energy spinning counter-clockwise from the base of my spine through the crown of my head. As I concentrated on the feeling, my spirit separated away from my body. The colors were dark as I gained my bearings. As the setting came into focus and light poured in over my right shoulder, I saw a non-descript female with dark shoulder-length hair and dark clothing look at me, retreat a few steps, and continue to retreat some more as if overpowered by what she saw.

When the setting first came into view, she appeared to be somehow a part of me – as if she had hijacked a ride on my soul and was not supposed to be there. I was greater in size, and the more everything came into focus, the greater in size my spirit became and forced her to retreat away. She looked at me as if she recognized that she was spiritually overpowered. I heard a word spoken over my shoulder. The word that rang out was "Ananda." Her facial expression is still engrained into my memory as she reacted in surprise to the spoken voice and

The Written (cont'd)

the size of my spirit. As she ran away, I felt a feeling of peace and tranquility overcome my body. I experienced this feeling for as long as I could hold harmony with the location, but eventually was forced to return to my earthly body.

As soon as I returned, I focused on departing again. I was able to re-engage and experience the vortex of energy in my spine again, but this time I decided to try something new – a technique that I have only understood conceptually through various oral resources. The technique I wanted to attempt was to split the double helical vortex into its two strands – to rip it open. Honestly I was not sure what the result would produce, but splitting the energy had been taught as how one can allow the spirit to manifest as a grand energy on Earth. I focused on how I would do this – though I do not know any technique beyond the concept. As I focused, I envisioned ripping apart the vortex. As I did this, I felt a great shock in the center of my chest and my earthly body spasmed in recognition of the splitting motion. The action was enough to feel like it took the air out of me which prevented me from finishing the technique that time. I do think that this is the first step in manifesting the energy, but it will require much discipline and practice in properly executing the technique.

So I awoke – startled, yet still with a grand feeling of tranquility and peace. I knew that the earlier interaction with Ananda had ridded my body of negative energy and allowed me to find a state of bliss. My prayer to God was asking for Him to help me understand where and why I was experiencing unusual negativity throughout my body today. Hosted

Rebirth II

negativity is a feeling I rarely ever experience – and I have not felt this particular feeling in quite a long time. So as I prayed, and the conversation went into motion, I understood the experience in the heavens to represent the negativity being ridded from my body. I also researched the name Ananda, for it seemed familiar. Indeed, it was the last of the three foundational words for the Brahman experience of Satchidānanda – the Sanskrit word I discovered after being imparted the word "chit" in a recent vision. Ananda (as a standalone word) means bliss. And certainly, that is what I experienced as being dispersed from my body.

December 28, 2013

Though the vision was brief, I was standing in a horizontal line with a large group of other followers of Christ. The setting seemed to be in the glory days of ancient Rome or ancient Greece. We were standing outside a gate that was the entrance into a city. The wall was sand colored, wide, tall, and thick. It seemed like it was at least several meters thick and at least twice the thickness in height. The gate had a large arch over the opening and thick, heavy doors that opened from the center. Their color was of dark walnut. The group I was with were all wearing white robes. Among the men, the hairstyles were all consistent – approximately shoulder length, wavy/curly and generally dark brown in color. The leader of the group asked the guard of the gate for entry into the city. I

The Written (cont'd)

had every sense that our leader was Christ-like, if not actually Jesus himself. It could have been Samson as well (since I identified Samson as Jesus in an earlier vision before I was corrected), but the distance prohibited me from clearly discerning his facial features.

As the man asked for entry, the guard held strong and denied him. The guard was large – a giant among men. He was wearing red cloth underneath his metallic armor. The leader of our group pleaded with the gatekeeper. He cried out, "If you will not allow us entry, then take us as your servants – as your slaves – so that we may enter the gates and serve you." And with those words, the massive doors to the gate swung open and the guard stepped aside (to our left side as we faced the gate). Our leader, said his thanks as we began to walk in and up a long cobblestone road. The guard said nothing and did not even have a change in his facial muscles. It was impressed upon me that our entrance into the gates was not because we were to be servants for those within, but rather that we showed humility upon entry and a willingness to serve God. It now appeared to me that our leader's plea to the guard for submission in servitude was not actually a plea to the guard, but rather a plea to God in demonstration of selfless humility and servitude unto Him. I awoke.

Rebirth II

December 29, 2013

The visions I experienced throughout the early morning hours on Earth were all uniquely different, but seem to have a storyline-arc that I have yet to fully put together. Last night, there were three visions, but the stories of each were woven together. It was as if each vision was a parallel timeline for my spiritual growth which I was able to experience by jumping from one to the next, to the next, and then returning to the previous timeline at will. It is worth noting that the settings were all once again very familiar – as if I had experienced them many times over, but have not fully been able to describe the visions, or retain the settings to journal upon returning to my earthly body. Though the visions were intertwined like a movie connecting multiple story lines, I will discuss each separately.

In the first vision a great angel was leading me around the outskirts of a city. The setting seemed post-apocalyptic, though I did not have a sense the area was in ruins or in disorder. It only appeared dirty and less refined than a pre-apocalyptic setting. The colors were shades of brown, red, and orange. There was a full palette of hues, but overall the setting just felt washed-out. The angel guide walked with me down a long road. To the left of the road was a river that was maybe twenty or thirty meters below the ground level. The setting was mostly dirt and clay – the road was made of small pebbles. As we walked, the angel continued to talk to me about the mysteries

The Written (cont'd)

of life and elaborate on many of the questions I have recently been asking. Though I did not feel like the discussion was opening up any new leaps in understanding, it was soothing to hear this holy voice.

During our walk, he pointed down to an object in the water. I gazed upon it, and I felt like it was the answer to my questions about the device to enable time travel. It was sitting in the water like a barge, but looked similar to a great earthmover used in modern construction. The object had a metallic cage and, surrounding the cage, six great wheels. The wheels might have been more appropriately called spheres, but the distance was too great to discern. They were definitely two-toned, though I think the inner tone illustrated a shape and the outer tone represented the body. The angel led me down and around the road until we eventually arrived at a loading dock at the base of the river. The dock was simple – wooden plank walkways on either side of a boat slip. The dock was covered with a large covering/awning to keep the weather out.

During our walk down the hill and to the left, the great object in the water fell out of view for a brief period. When we walked to the edge of the dock, I gazed upon the waters and saw that the object was now being hoisted by a crane. It was bent in the middle and the crane's clamps continued to crush the object. I felt sad, frustrated that I could not thoroughly see and understand the object's architecture. While the object seemed to be an unlikely candidate (in form) for the time travel device, I knew upon seeing it that the device held within it great truths. I am not sure that the form itself was indicative of

Rebirth II

what needs to be built, but rather an indication of the mechanical principles to be used in the device.

As I saw the object being crushed, I also noticed that the wheels were indeed more spherical in nature. The two tones of color seemed to indicate a vortex created within each sphere – like the apple design I have seen when researching the Meru Foundation. I was not able to form words to ask the angel about the destruction. My emotions held me frozen in the moment. Perhaps I was only supposed to witness the construct of the object and not be able to ask questions. Perhaps it was my own inability to hold harmony with the moment. Either way, the object is entrenched in my mind, through which the design spoke mechanical truths and principles.

The second vision was a return to the prison setting I have experienced in the past. This time, I was able to understand the setting with more depth and clarity. I believe the term "prison" may be more appropriately called "holding facility" where it is more of a construct in the restriction of action and access to some thing or some particular information. The workers all were dressed more like orderlies in a hospital than what I would expect to see in a prison. They all wore blue scrubs. As I found myself in this prison setting, I realized once again that my phone had been taken from me upon entry. I felt strongly compelled that I needed to call someone and let them know where I was.

The last time I was in this setting, I thought there were only eight days left on this "sentence" – so my spirit was strongly confused as to why I was still in the prison. I felt like I

The Written (cont'd)

was only there out of a technicality – that I had ridden in the passenger's seat of a car of someone who was apparently intoxicated (I only discovered this later upon being taken to this center). I wandered over to the front desk where a receptionist seemed very distracted. I asked her a few questions that caused her to put a bag containing my possessions on her desk as I filled out forms. When she turned her back, I grabbed my phone out of the bag and a phone number on a torn sheet of paper that, for some reason, I felt was important. When she turned back to me, I handed her my paperwork and returned to the holding room. I eventually decided I needed to get out – not escape per se – but just leave the premises to clear my mind. I found a door and walked out.

While I had been in the prison, I overheard people talking about my backstory. For some reason I had decided not to let anyone know upon admittance into the prison that I had left my vehicle unattended on a street a great distance away. I decided that it was important to go check on my vehicle. I walked a great distance through a misty rain down through several city blocks, eventually arriving in a parking garage. I looked for my vehicle, but it was nowhere to be seen. I wanted to call the number on the paper I had brought with me, but felt that by doing so I would be breaking some unwritten law that I had to fend for myself. I resisted the call. Eventually, I decided I needed to return to the prison.

When I entered, I realized no one had missed me at all. No one had even realized I had been gone. The only indication I had from anyone was a nurse that looked at me as I

Rebirth II

entered through the front doors. Her facial expression seemed to indicate confusion as to why I was coming in through the front door. I eased her mind by telling her I was returning and had to step away for a minute. She seemed content and went about her way. When I entered through the doors, everyone was decorating for a New Year's party. All of their attention was on the celebration and not on the people in the prison. I realized I needed to use the restroom so I headed down through a large empty room and over to a bathroom in the back right corner. I still had my phone with me and decided it was probably best I figure out a way to hide it.

When I reached the bathroom, a female worker in scrubs directed me into a small room. I used the restroom and exited. I asked the lady why I was there. The more I tried to rationalize the scenario, the more it did not make any sense. She told me I was there for "trying to do too much." I asked her how many days I had left on my sentence and she responded by telling me "twenty days." I was shocked, surprised and extremely disappointed inside. I asked her when my sentence changed from eight days to twenty, but all she could tell me was that it had always been twenty days. She was unsure where I heard eight days at all. As I wrestled with the thought, I fell out of harmony with the location.

When I opened my eyes, I felt impressed that there was a strong significance in the vision and corresponding moon phases. I am not quite sure why my brain went to moon phases, but I decided to check the phases for 2014. For the past couple of years, I have noticed a strong correlation of the half

The Written (cont'd)

moon to the intensities of the visions I have experienced. Recently, I have begun to wonder if a waning or waxing half moon makes a difference. So, it came as no surprise when I checked the 2014 calendar to see that eight days from New Year is a half moon, and twenty days from New Year is a half moon. The half moon that appears eight days after New Year is waxing. The half moon that begins to appear twenty days (twenty-two days precisely) after New Year is waning. There are two days left in 2013, so that is why the twenty days should be observed as relative to my question to the orderly, but my answer to her about eight days should be seen as finite in regard to the day indicated by the New Year's celebration decorations. Also, this is the first time I have ever realized that there are twenty-two days precisely between half moons. This is extremely important because there are twenty-two archetypes of the mind so the phases can now be equated to the archetypes.

    My third and final vision is one that I struggled including in this journal, but since I have been transparent and all-inclusive of every other vision to date, it is important that I include this as well. As I have been on my personal journey, I have had to learn to separate myself from ego. As any human is subjected to the trials and tribulations of earthly desires, I too struggled with the concepts. I began phasing out different nuances in my life that I felt could lead me astray. A major stumbling block for me had been in relationships. After my divorce I felt like my spirit had become encumbered by a

Rebirth II

granite casing that no one would be able to get through. The granite casing was the protection to my heart and soul.

My divorce crushed me – though I know that my ego was in denial of the inevitable ending developing during the last half of our marriage. This does not resolve the fact that I did not allow anyone else access to my heart, but it is important to understand this part of my history. So during the next several years I dated without thoughts of commitment. Eventually, when I found myself in the darkness that surrounded my thirtieth birthday (the darkness that I can define as the true beginning of my rebirth), I began to filter out the noise from my life in order to focus on self-discovery and God.

During the journey, I realized that the social part of my life was a distraction and inhibitor of my development, so I cut that part of my life out. I realized that relationships were an exercise in futility so I cut that part of my life out as well. I put everything I once was on the table for God to help me sort out; I had to do so in the steps that he asked of me. As relationships and interactions with women fell from my life, I turned to adult videos to help keep my mind grounded – at least that was my justification. I was aware that it was only a crutch and eventually turned to God for help. After continual prayer in asking for strength, I was able to completely remove that aspect from my life. This left me naked, my soul bare. Earthly desires were placed on a shelf while I continued to develop spiritually. This was the end and the beginning. I was no longer who I was, but who I was to become.

The Written (cont'd)

My body experienced some mentally perplexing situations during this time. Eighteen months had passed since I had even kissed a woman, and my body reacted to that absence erratically. No doubt this was at least partly due to a shift in hormonal balance I was experiencing. There were large periods of time I felt nothing sexual at all. Previously being a man of extremely intense carnal desires, this has been a mental roller coaster for me. I have had to have faith that all of it had a purpose in reconditioning my body into a more whole representation of my spiritual center.

As I have worked out and retooled my physique, my sexual drive would come in bursts and then subside. Much of it had to do with removing the visual imagery I was exposed to from the videos. I became reliant on the image rather than the emotion. Sex is an act of unity, and through the exposure to the adult industry, sex had become an act of ego – an act of gratification. I know that this reconditioning was bringing me back to my origin. In the beginning, when I first met my ex-wife, I had waited for the right woman before I had sex. I recall wanting it to always be an act of "making Love" and not "having sex." Though I wanted sex all of the time, all day long, I always saw it as an act of spiritual unity. To the ears of most people on Earth, "making Love" is a cringe-worthy term, for most are lost to the carnal desires. But I always saw it differently.

Through the years after my divorce, this mental purity was long lost due to the granite casing around my heart and soul. My pessimism toward Love grew uncontrollably and un-

Rebirth II

knowingly to me. So, while that is a large backstory to this vision, it is important to realize that I originally had a spiritual recognition of sex as an act of divine unity, but in the years after my divorce I had lost focus – lost touch with the spiritual aspects of it. This is why sex can become a distraction to those on a spiritual journey. It was placed here by God to be used in recognition of spiritual unity, not of purely carnal (ego) satisfaction. In all things good, ego can still take charge and cause darkness to take root. So while this is a large backstory, it is important to bring us to the present moment.

Nearly five years ago after becoming recently divorced, I met a girl who was in a similar situation as I. She was in a new relationship though – one that would last until the recent months. At the time, we had a great conversation, but timing was definitely not right for either of us to attempt pursuing anything. Her soul touched mine the moment I saw her eyes, though I would never even ask for her number. Throughout the years we have stayed in touch through various social networks, and it was only in the recent weeks that we started communicating again. She invited me to church with her and I have obliged to go next weekend. Honestly I am looking extremely forward to it and I hope that the last eighteen months have not put me too far out of practice from making my nerves appear non-existent, where I would only radiate an ease and confidence in speech and mannerisms.

I am admittedly nervous – which I understand is my ego interfering. But, I am also extremely calm and collected spiritually. The recent conversations with her have caused me to

The Written (cont'd)

review the growth and strides I have made over the years. Though I am not sure how this will turn out, I always have an optimism that defeats the strongest doubter. But this time, I know that it is spiritual – it is all in God's hands. I place the next part of the journey in Him as I learn to walk again in a new friendship, perhaps a new relationship. As doubts have filled my mind, I have prayed for God to offer guidance and strength. The mental roller-coaster I have experienced from rebuilding the understanding of my sex drive and carnal desires has only introduced anxiety into my daily life. So, I find it interesting that the next vision would play into that part of my life. The premise was simple – the message concise.

In this vision I was being escorted through a location with muted scenery. With the angel, I discussed my fear that I had lost touch with my sexual drive and that it would prohibit me from balancing the act of my spiritual and earthly walk in a relationship. Obviously sex is important in a relationship, and I still strongly mentally desire the carnal side of Love and long to have my heart wide open again. But, the ups and downs in my sex drive have introduced doubts into my mind. The angel spoke not in words, but led me to a room. In the room a beautiful girl was laying naked on a stone table. Her body was glowing – radiating light. The angel was on my left. I was viewing her on the table from the right portion of the room.

The table was facing mostly lengthwise towards me, but angled enough so I could see her whole figure. Her left knee was raised 45° upward. Her right leg was bent at a 45° angle, but resting on its side across the stone table. Her left hand

Rebirth II

reached above the back of her head grasping for anything to hold on to. Her right hand was between her legs as she began to pleasure herself. She writhed in pleasure from the stimulation her fingers were providing. I was forced to watch this for approximately a minute or so. The angel would not let me turn away. While she was pleasuring herself, the angel spoke in stern words: "The way you are to reactivate your sex drive is to masturbate as many times a day as you can." As the words resonated within, my mind raced at the radical nature of this vision. Truthfully, it flies in the face of many spiritual teachings. I had most certainly been told on a spiritual level how to reactivate my sex drive for my earthly walk. I have to believe, though, that this allowance to rekindle my sex drive is, in part, due to my spiritual growth so far – my recognition of sex as an expression of unity.

I know I was led astray during the time after my divorce, but I was now back on the right track. The removal of the imagery for my carnal desires helped me to find my spiritual desire within the carnal desire. It makes me no less sexual in nature than the next – but rather more sexual in that the carnal desire streaks past the ego and straight to the spirit. As I contemplated the thoughts, the implications, my mind raced and I lost harmony with the vision.

And while I do not normally add additional perspective to the messages provided by the angels, I feel that this specific message should be treated with much more delicacy than many of the other messages I have received. I think that it is important to note that any words added do introduce a slight

The Written (cont'd)

bias to the divine message being revealed, but it is coming from a perspective that I hope will be received in a way that will allow the lesson to remain uncolored. All of this particular experience has been relayed in an unfiltered and unabridged manner – as difficult as it was for me to include due to the subject matter. But that is the important part of this writing. The lessons I have received have all been part of a journey far grander than each experience in and of itself.

So with that said, I think it is important to not view the message received as a reason to justify gratification of self. In all aspects of life there is one single question that should always be asked: Does this action glorify God or does it serve to entertain the ego? And while the meaning of that question to the message received may not be readily apparent, it is important to explore every circumstance surrounding the situation and realize the message – just like every other message in this book – is applicable for a given situation, a given intention, all within the given circumstances.

As it will be revealed later in my journals, there is a fine line between a lesson and a test. At this point along my journey, I did not necessarily understand that divide, but I also cannot tell you if God had introduced that particular divide into His lessons for me yet. All I know is the situation presented in the moment and the eventual destination I find myself in today in regard to this particular subject matter. And – perhaps – that may be the most important aspect to explore. For as these books take their final form during the first few months of 2015, it is easy to see how the lesson was applicable to the

Rebirth II

journey at a micro level and a macro level. In the immediate moment, they held meaning. In hindsight, they held sustenance and glue for the story being told. For if the words in these Books of Nine are received and viewed as an ideal to strive toward throughout each person's personal journey, then it should be viewed in the complete context of past, present, and future. The lesson received on December 29, 2013, is part of a greater story being told, and that is the most important aspect to the lesson of the angel's words.

December 30, 2013

While I had several visions last night, there is only one that I can recall with great depth. These visions all echoed a familiar setting – as if they have been recurring, and I have just been unable to retain the information each time they occurred. In each of the other visions, I never quite found harmony and could not willfully interact with the scenarios. When I tried to do so, it caused me to fall out of the vision and lose memory of the surroundings. However, the one that I can recall in detail dealt with a large portion of land.

This land was being divided up among a group of people. The angelic leader of the group told me I would be given a smaller portion, but indicated it would be of greater significance. Initially, the group divided up the land by consensus – where I received the smallest portion of the land that was unwanted by the individuals. There was another individual who

The Written (cont'd)

was to receive a similarly small portion, but I did not have any interaction with that person. When I explored the land given to me, I found it to be lush with vegetation. The land also had a small, running brook through the middle of the property. The angel asked me if I was satisfied. I wanted to explore the other parts of the land to make sure I could see why I was given that portion. When I explored the land, the angel told me that my property was part of something significant. I felt that the value of everyone else's land contained a larger portion of whatever this significant feature may be (assuming it ran through the land and was divided accordingly), so I was surprised to see that my land also was part of this significance. I tried to ask more questions about the land, but I knew my time was drawing to a close. I returned to my earthly body with possibly more questions than I had answers from the vision.

December 31, 2013

Throughout the night I again experienced many fantastical visions. However, I think because I was trying too hard to find harmony during them, it had the adverse reaction of causing me to lose harmony and recollection of the events. This is very similar to the concept of "do without doing" and "mind of no mind." Sometimes it is easy to get lost while attempting to be found. Regardless, I did have one extremely clear vision to write about. This vision involved another familiar setting.

Rebirth II

Somewhere in the deep heart of a thick, aged forest, there is (what I can only describe as) a training camp/boot camp for people of my similar spiritual capability. I can only describe it as a form of spiritual boot camp where obstacles and physical training help bring the mind and spirit into better control and harmony with the surroundings. I have been here multiple times before, though I am unsure if I have written about the experiences. My vision began in this location outside of a large cabin. I think this cabin was the main part of the school. I am extremely confident it is the same cabin that I wrote about in a previous vision where I observed the rafters and skylights/windows high above the grand floor.

When the vision began, I was outside of this building and running on a trail. The trail wound around and through the forest. The trees towered hundreds of feet above me. In earthly terms, the trees were the type that can be found in mountain forests that have been protected from human habitation for thousands upon thousands of years. As I ran, I felt peace. There was not a sense of struggle or frustration which I normally feel when I run in my earthly body. My strides were short and somewhat awkward, but I assumed it was because I was carrying a cup in either hand filled with water. In my left hand, I held a glass with ice water slushing about. In my right hand I held a paper cup with a lid and a straw. It also contained water – though without the ice. As I ran I became aware that the glass with water was for my consumption to prevent dehydration. The cup in my right hand was to prevent overheating. These two cups served two distinctly different

The Written (cont'd)

purposes, though they held the same type of water (as far as I could tell).

As I jogged over a hill, I heard an instructor far off in the distance shouting out to all of the trainees, "Don't forget to drink your water. It is important to make sure that everyone drinks their water." I decided I needed to take a swig of water from the glass in my left hand. As I crested the hill on my jog, the sun poured through the trees. I could not tell if it was a sunset or a sunrise, but the sun was in that type of low position in the sky. I put the glass to my lips and took two large sips from the water. As I did so, I heard two older teenagers standing to the side of the trail say, "Uh oh. He's already drinking the water. He's not going to make it." They continued to laugh and make jokes about me drinking the water. It was not insulting – more like teammates giving another teammate a hard time to help them become stronger and better at their position.

I ran down the hill feeling a little humiliated, but not in the way I would ever use that term on Earth. I was disappointed in myself. I wanted to push myself harder. As I rounded the first lap of the trail that ended with the cabin on my right, I noticed the instructor standing to the left. When I ran by him I tried to hand him my glass of water. He looked surprised and asked me why I was giving it to him. I told him that I did not need it – I just needed the one that kept me from overheating. As soon as I handed the glass over to him, my feet became extremely heavy and I tripped and fell to the ground. I tried to get up, but my feet felt weighted down to the ground. The in-

Rebirth II

structor just watched to see what I would do. I managed to stand up. When I looked at my feet, I saw that I was running with large dumbbells strapped to the bottom of my feet. When I saw this, I was confused why this was the case, but also rationalized it as to why my stride felt awkward earlier. I gathered my composure and began to try to run. With each step I had to concentrate harder and harder to lift each foot from the ground and place it in front of the other. I chugged forward on the track at a snails pace – though I was moving forward. Somewhere in the process the strenuous nature of the effort overtook my concentration and I lost harmony with the location.

As I awoke I realized that the weights on my feet were likely more of a visual manifestation of a thought. I am not sure there were truly weights attached to my feet or if that was my mind rationalizing the feeling of not being able to move freely about. The major challenge with visions is interpreting truth from concepts, and trusting that God is communicating with me in a manner that I will be able to understand. For me, the concept of the weights means much more than whether the weights were real or not. For if they were real, or just a concept, they still represented the same message – an archetypal meaning that spoke to my spirit in terms of my spiritual and physical growth.

I was definitely being trained. The water for hydration was equally as important as the water to prevent overheating. When I tried to run without the glass of water, I lost focus on not spilling the water while I ran and therefore was overcome

The Written (cont'd)

with the awareness of my astral body in motion. Yes, I am learning to run. I am sure that my spirit is receiving some sort of a boot camp to help me get into shape to better navigate the heavens. I also believe that the spiritual boot camp has an effect in my earthly walk as well. The stronger that I become in the spiritual realm, the more centered I become in the earthly realm.

My body has experienced a swath of emotions in the recent weeks since Lindsey (a girl who I had once met several years prior) reached out to me. I know God told me to "tread lightly" when I first decided to move forward with it, and I believe that is because my spirit is still like unto a child. I am experiencing hormones and emotions that I have not experienced since I was physically a youth going through puberty. Every feeling is a roller coaster of emotions. That is not to say that I am an emotional wreck, or anything similar. But it is to demonstrate an entirely new understanding of my spirit and my body interacting with one another.

I originally thought that "seeing the world though the eyes of a child" was pretty much set on an absolute scale. I now see it to be relative. For as a child sees the world, it changes with age. A child's body changes to adapt to its surroundings. There are hormonal changes within the body producing roller coasters of emotions that are enough to drive a youth to do extreme things. The body is controlled by the emotions. My place on Earth today is not unlike that same experience – but through the lens of the spirit. To be re-birthed unto the Lord our Father in Heaven, is to be humbled like unto a baby. The growth that has occurred is like that of a child's growth. And now, I am being allowed to feel; to feel the ocean of emotions that roll throughout the human body in a way a pubescent teen first feels those emotions.

The spiritual boot camp is a type of calibration for my spirit. Just as I need to advance and grow in the spiritual realm so that I can better navigate the heavens and effortlessly blend my spiritual body between two worlds, I also have to center, refine and chisel away at the wildness of human emotions. Advancing spiritually will bring peace unto the chaotic tide of emotions. It is like a spiritual yoke whereby the emotions are experienced just as they are as a pubescent teen, but bound to the spirit so that the emotions never feel like they are in control of the body but are yoked to the strength of spirit. Today I feel more yoked at my center, and I have to assume this feeling will only get stronger as I grow through my spiritual journey in the heavens.

January 1, 2014

In the same pattern of previous nights, I again had multiple visions – each difficult to recall. The main vision I can recall was the final vision of the evening. I appeared in the heavens with a man snapping his fingers. The snap was extraordinarily loud. When he noticed he had caught my attention, the man said, "I suppose I didn't need to snap quite that loudly – now did I?" I snickered and told him, "No. You

The Written (cont'd)

managed to snap really loudly though. That was impressive." We laughed for a brief second. The man was older with gray hair. He was very tall and impressively built. I knew he was an elder of the angels, but I did not know who he was. This was the first time I had observed this man with enough detail to bring the vision back to Earth with me.

As I gathered my bearings, I realized I was standing with another couple. At first they seemed like they were wanderers – spirits without recognition of their location. The man led us all to an event being thrown at a large house. When we arrived, the couple decided they were very hungry. I agreed that I could eat as well so we wandered through the house looking for some food. When we were inside, the girl (who seemed at this point to have gathered control of her spirit) started explaining a food that she ate the last time she was here. She was really excited about it. She kept describing it as "like a crispy noodle" but it was not a noodle I would have ever had before.

We began a quest to find this food. She and I wandered through the house and out the back door. It was raining and dark. In front of us was a sectioned off area of land that was used for crops. It was small – maybe only a thousand square feet. Above the entire section were tents to keep the rain from damaging the crops. In the garden was a keeper. This keeper was "the girl" that continued to show up in all of my visions. But for simplicity in distinguishing between the other girl I was with, I will refer to her as the garden keeper in this vision. When she saw us, she greeted us and welcomed us into the garden. We asked her if any of the type of food we were

Rebirth II

searching for was in the garden. She smiled and said there was and motioned over to the back left corner of the garden. She walked the girl and me over to it. As I walked into the section, I heard a crunching sound from the ground. I looked down but initially only saw a few yellowish/golden specs glowing before me. I understood those glowing specs to be seeds that had yet to flower/take root in the garden. I was not quite sure what I could be walking on that would be crushed beneath my feet. I reached down and ran my hand over the ground. As I did, I could tell the ground was filled with glittering transparent crystals.

The keeper indicated the food we sought were the crystals beneath my feet and told me I could have as much as I wanted. The girl I was with wanted me to try this food. I tasted it, and while I do not recall the taste in detail, I recognized its fulfillment within me. I also enjoyed the texture of what I was eating. It was sweet, like a dessert, but that is all I could understand. The girl was so excited and wandered off eating some of the crystals she had scooped off the ground of the garden.

The keeper handed me a plate. She knew I was going to be more refined in how I took the food back with me. I reached onto the ground and scooped up the crystals and piled them on my plate. I wanted to get enough to give some to the guy that we arrived with (the girl's boyfriend, as was my impression). I kept piling more and more on the plate, but the portion did not continue to grow past a certain point. I felt that it was not quite enough for two people, so I continued trying to add more. Every time I did, I watched the food on the

The Written (cont'd)

plate melt away into a puddle. It was as if the amount of matter on my plate was limited before it changed texture to liquid. I eventually began to get a little frustrated, and looked at the keeper and asked her if I had enough for two people. She smiled and said I did. I replied, "Okay. I just wanted to check. I can't seem to put anymore on the plate and I wanted to make sure I had enough for the other guy with us." She just smiled and assured me I would be okay.

    I returned inside the house. I gave the plate of food to the guy that was with us and then decided to go back outside. I wandered through the garden and crested a hill. There was a lake before me. The lake had a peculiar quality though. I sensed danger, or evil in the lake. I walked to the shore and saw a snake swim to the surface of the lake and begin to swim toward me. I knew that I was in a dangerous area and wondered how many things existed in the lake that could cause harm. As I began to retreat, the snake increased the speed of its approach. As it neared the shore, I heard a loud crash. A tree fell before me dividing me from the lake. I knew at once that the fallen tree had saved me. But, I was still unclear as to what was trying to harm me.

    As I began to walk away, I heard the sound of a whimper. I walked back to the tree and noticed a large, hideous boar lying on its side crushed by the tree. I knew it would not survive. I wondered if this was a test. I decided to seek out the teacher to see if I was supposed to help the boar's spirit transition on painlessly, or if I was supposed to let it suffer. I walked back to the garden, but the keeper was no longer there. I

Rebirth II

walked inside and learned that the group wanted to be taken to another place. I obliged since I appeared to be the most coherent in the group. As we left we said goodbye to the man that greeted me with the snaps when we arrived.

Though I cannot recall where we went specifically or why we left, I do know we returned very quickly. The distance we had to travel was not very far. Once we returned, we entered through the building's lobby. I went to the restroom and came out. When I came out, the man who had earlier snapped passed by. He looked at me extremely surprised, but with happiness. He asked, "I thought you had to go?" I replied, "Oh. We already left and came back. It was a short trip – just right down the road." The man seemed confused but extremely happy on all counts of us returning. He invited us back in. As we headed back in, I lost harmony with the vision and fell back to Earth.

January 2, 2014

Last night the visions again came in three. The first was short, and occurred during meditation before falling asleep. I simply was standing in a garden and I realized there was an insect flying near me. It continued to fly around me. I ducked and tried to avoid it. I was not fearful of the insect, but it was mostly annoying me. As I stood there, I realized there were more insects in the distance. I suddenly realized this was how I first heard the primordial sound as it began to ring out louder.

The Written (cont'd)

I became excited that I was again experiencing this phenomenon, and my mind began to race. Keeping with tradition over the last week, the more my mind began to race, the more the vision began to fade. I awoke from the meditation.

The second vision's setting was in a cafeteria. It was lighted with muted colors. I was standing in a long line for food. As I waited in line, I began rationalizing why I was standing there. This was my spiritual body and earthly body finding harmony in the moment. Over the course of a couple of minutes, I realized that I was in my spiritual body.

As I came to that recognition, a man who appeared to be in his twenties came in. He immediately recognized me and walked over to say hi. He was very short with curly hair. As we waited in line, another guy whom I recognized came up and stood in line with us. He was also very short. To put it in perspective, I would say I was nearly twice the height of these people. My earthly mind tried attaching names of people I knew to the spirits. While most of the time I recognize when my mind attempts to rationalize to whom I am talking, this time was different. I could not tell if I was really experiencing interactions with their earthly spirits or if I was rationalizing the heavenly unknown. For the sake of this journal entry, I will not attach the names to the spirits.

What made this interaction different was the number of spirits that seemed familiar. It was as if I was interacting with many people that I knew in my city. In the scheme of heavenly principles, earthly interactions are relative in location to All That Is in the heavens, so it would make sense these were the

Rebirth II

souls of people I knew. But, outside of my closest friends, I have not ever recognized I was in the true presence of a soul of someone I only socially knew. But I digress.

We made it through the line and sat down at a table. The stool I sat on was taller than the table's height. I required that large of a stool for my body size. We joked about the size of the stool in relation to their heights. I did not feel like a giant, nor did they seem short to me. I could only acknowledge the difference in relativity. As we ate, I sat at the head of the table. I asked if anyone noticed another guy who walked in earlier. I made sure they knew they were in the presence of someone of greatness. One of the guys at my table said he did notice and explained the circumstances surrounding what he witnessed. I felt like a teacher – a leader – though I did not feel the ego usually attached to one.

As we ate, a girl stood behind me. She started speaking over my right shoulder. Those at our table had been making small talk, and someone mentioned not feeling well. The girl said, "Oh, you mean like Stacey (my ex-wife) would get sick every time you came near her during her pregnancy." I knew not what she meant in her sentence, but my soul agreed with her. I am pretty confident that she was indicating the battle between the righteous and someone still struggling to accept their spirituality. It would seem that my ex wife's negativity toward me during her pregnancy was due to a spiritual struggle and not the hormonal struggle of pregnancy.

As she spoke, I turned to look at her. She had my attention. She was gorgeous. She was one of the sandy-blonde

The Written (cont'd)

angels that I see regularly. Her face did not have strong features, but she was regal and mesmerizing. I felt a strong attraction to her. I wanted to call her by the name Hayden (and have every other time I have seen her), but I did not know where this name had stemmed from. As my eyes fell into hers, she said she was going to go make some coffee. I followed her to get a refill on the water I was drinking (my impression was this was a substance to keep me from overheating).

As we waited in line, I sat on the stool I had with me at the table. She went on and made her coffee and rounded a corner heading toward another room. After I refilled my water, I walked over to her. She asked if I wanted some. I said I was okay. She led me into a room adjacent to the cafeteria where there was a large bed. She sat on it like a child wanting to share stories with a good friend. I hopped in the bed with her. We were both barefoot. I pulled the comforter over my legs as we sat and talked. She was facing me and eventually readjusted her legs under the comforter. When she did so, she intentionally brushed her foot across mine to make contact. Her foot was smooth and cold – like cold feet in a bed. The sensation of our feet touching ignited me inside.

She led the conversation. She wanted to talk about her impression of the experiences I have had on Earth. She asked, "So, when you go out, most of the time they don't give you anything in return. I mean, no gifts, nothing special – no recognition. Even just a simple thank you would be nice. But they don't even do that, do they?" I tried to figure out the context of her question and decided she was talking about people

Rebirth II

in the service industry being rude to customers. I laughed and said, "Well it depends where you go. When I first got divorced I went out a lot on Broadway." She smiled – impressed. "Broadway? Really?" she asked. I said, "Of course. It was quite fun at the time, but isn't something I do much (if ever) at all anymore." "Why?" she asked. "Where do you like to go?" She gave me a look like, "Nice try." We laughed.

    I began explaining about some of my other experiences and where I went on Earth. I began talking about the fun I had with my friends when I was first divorced. But as I talked, I was careful about everything I said. I could not quite decide what might make me look bad in her eyes (though it may have been fun for me). This was an interesting change of thought because on Earth, the reminiscing of stories is always socially acceptable, regardless of how someone may have been judged at the time. On Earth, people judge at the time of an action, but laugh about stories past. In this moment I could not discern what was socially acceptable to tell her. She wanted to know everything about my experiences, but I wanted to make sure I did not look like I had faltered along the way – though falters did lead to eventual successes. I thought more deeply about each word that came out of my mouth. As we talked, my thought process deepened to a point that it pulled me out of harmony with the location and my spirit returned to Earth. I tried to return to her, but was unable to traverse back.

    The third vision occurred in a setting that I have experienced at least once before. I was in a great office building preparing for a presentation I was to give. The last time I was

The Written (cont'd)

in this setting, I procrastinated until the last minute but managed to give a stellar presentation, despite the odds of it going poorly. This time everything felt different. It seemed like time had passed, and I had advanced in growth during the gap since the last time I was there. As I sat in the room, I found my customary position at the head of the table. But the way the table was shaped, it was more like the head-corner.

I sat back in my chair confidently, but at ease. Everyone else seemed very tense. They began talking about many different business-esque subjects and continued to turn to me for answers. I was able to give answers based on my earthly experiences in the business world. There was one point that I was asked a specific question regarding the health and wellbeing of others. The question was asked by whom I perceived as the "headmaster" – a lady who was stern, well educated, had short hair, wore glasses, and was superior to all of the others in the room, including me.

As I gave an answer based on my earthly experience, everyone became extremely attentive to the solution I had shared. They immediately turned to each other and began discussing how to use the answer I had given in practical terms within their business practices. I am still not sure what the specifics of their business practices were, but I know that it dealt with the health and well being of others – possibly spirits, possibly another race, possibly earthly bodies. The mind can spin at the possibilities of what the true meaning of what I experienced could actually be. But, instead of allowing my mind to race, I held my composure.

Rebirth II

After I had given my answer, we broke for lunch. Over lunch, I decided that I could take my time to return. I wandered about the property and the building while observing all I could. I had conversations with a few others and eventually returned to the building. Our meeting room had changed. Also, during this portion of the meeting, I was supposed to give the presentation I had been preparing for earlier. I entered the room and set my laptop down on the table. One of the others in the room tried to pull up some information on it, but needed another application to do so. I let him go ahead and install what he needed. It was going to take a few minutes, so I wandered out of the room and out of the building.

Outside, the sun was shining brightly. This was the first experience I had had with blue skies in the heavens. Almost every other time the settings had been at night or at dawn/dusk. As I observed the sky, I breathed the air in deeply. With each breath, the surroundings became more vivid. The building I had exited was one of two identical buildings on the property. These buildings faced each other, but were separated by a large, well-manicured lawn with well-groomed shrubbery. There was a sidewalk that connected the two buildings with a large fountain between. As I soaked in the scenery, I turned to my left and saw a road in the distance. I was viewing the road on its perpendicular axis.

As I watched the traffic on the road pass by, I saw a dog run across the road, cutting through traffic and toward me. It was a beautiful dog. Its coat was a light beige with curly hair (like a golden-doodle's coat). The dog was medium sized, like a

The Written (cont'd)

golden retriever or small lab. I called out to the dog by name, "Nah-Nah." The dog made it safely across the street and ran into my arms. I knew I had "saved" the dog from being injured from the traffic. I walked back into the building, down a hallway, and into an adjacent room to the presentation room. Others were gathered in this room to observe the presentation I was to give in the other room. There was a glass window separating the two rooms.

When I entered the room, everyone was astounded that I had saved a dog. On top of my successes in the meeting before lunch, as well as the opportunity in the presentation I was about to give, I had also saved a puppy. I told everyone the dog's name was "Nah-Nah." But each time I said the name, I felt like I had a hard time pronouncing it – as if I could not quite get the articulation correct. Though the syllable-tones were correct, the enunciation and inflections were equally important in getting the name correct. Though unsatisfied that I never said the name correctly, everyone around me accepted what I said without question. After a few minutes of waiting in the room with the puppy, I heard my name called. I walked out of the room with the dog in my arms and into the hallway.

In the distance a couple was walking toward me in a blinding light. The man was on my left – the ladies right. He wore a white suit and had black, slicked back hair and a well-manicured beard. He held a cigar in his hand. On his left, was a female (I took to be his girlfriend/wife). She wore a stunning white dress. She was shorter than he. If he was seven feet tall, she was maybe a foot to a foot and a half shorter than that.

Rebirth II

She had long, medium-light brown hair with golden streaks highlighting the reflections from the light illuminating them from behind. They each smiled at me, glad to see that their dog was safe. They were extremely familiar to me, but seemed somewhat elusive to meet on a regular basis in the heavens. It seemed like a special moment of reuniting with friends that I have not seen in a while.

When they approached me, I handed the dog over to the girl. They were happy to see the dog, but almost unsurprised. The man asked where I found the dog. I explained that it had run across the highway into my arms, and that I had saved it from being hit. They laughed at each other giving me the impression this happens pretty often. The man turned to the girl and said, "Well, I guess he spent the day at Joe's bar." The girl then explained that sometimes the dog wanders over to the bar to stay with all of the patrons. They were extremely thankful that I had found their dog, though. We eventually said our goodbyes, and I headed back into the main room to give my presentation. Though I cannot recount the details of the presentation, I know that the presentation went extremely well. I know I talked about my earthly experiences and how they intertwined with their business intentions.

After the presentation, I was given a tremendous number of compliments. I could also hear the small talk about me behind my back. The conversation was about how great I was becoming – and I had even saved a puppy to boot. Saving the puppy was like a cliché that actually occurred in their presence

The Written (cont'd)

and, thus, continued to build respect for whatever it was that I was contributing to their cause.

After the meeting, I walked upstairs with a group. One of the ladies from the presentation earlier asked me to come with her into another room. When I entered, there were two other women already in the room. The room was very small – barely large enough for us to fit in and have room to move our arms. The room had pictures stapled on the walls, small round mirrors on the shelves, and was in disarray with hair curlers and hair products. The two girls that were already in the room when we entered were curling their hair. Everyone was excited to see me. The girls all chatted back and forth for some time. I just sat there, unsure of my purpose in the room. I just continued to observe all of the pictures on the wall in front of me – my back to the girls.

Every now and then I would contribute something to the conversation, but the conversation turned more into a "girl conversation" where they were talking about girl issues, etc. I felt strongly out of place and joked about how I should perhaps leave so they could keep talking about their girl problems, because I was not going to be able to contribute to the conversation. As I said that, one of the girls came up behind me and embraced me from behind. Her hair was wild and in disarray – sticking out in all curly directions from her head. I felt her head bury itself into my neck and back, her hair crushing around me. She was an older woman – not attractive to me in the way some of the other women had been. As she held me she said, "I'm so sorry for not seeing. I thought you were just

Rebirth II

going to be another drunk boozing it up. I heard the stories and just assumed you were going to be like the others. But they were right about you."

My mind raced at what she said. As she continued to talk, I began to understand that what she meant was that in my earthly experiences, the nights out drinking with friends had the great potential for failure. I now was not sure which world was real. Was it the earthly experience that was real and the visions were a way to guide and shape my spirit, or was the earthly experience just a way to grow my spirit for another alternate reality? As I pondered the thought, the girl continued to embrace me from behind. She emphasized over and over how much she originally disliked me and had so much disdain for me when I was introduced to everyone. But then she said something that sent shockwaves throughout my body.

"I now see what everyone else sees in you. You are special. You can do things that others have been unable to do. Everyone else saw hope in your potential. I just thought you would be another drunk. But I was so wrong. I now see it. I now see what everyone else sees." Her words echoed throughout the depths of my soul. The feeling was so deep, that I lost harmony with the moment and returned to my earthly body.

I suppose it is also important to note that I have not had anything to drink over the last month – and rarely anything over the last year. Even as the holidays generally usher in times of celebration, I have chosen to abstain from it recently. Somehow, I have recognized it is not the alcohol that affects me negatively, but the exposure of my soul to the polarizations

The Written (cont'd)

of the earthly walk that have the potential to affect my growth negatively. This does not mean there will not be a day when I understand how to manage alcohol, but for now, it is necessary to abstain during my rebirth. It is now obvious that I am in uncharted territory from where others may have traversed before me. Somehow, someway – I am building a bridge between peoples – people unknown to me where they exist in the universe, time, spirit, or relativity to my earthly walk.

Over the last week, I have come to accept there must be multiple spiritual timelines that are all interacting with each other simultaneously – in ways greater than I can comprehend. The last week of visions has been the most intense week of my life. This vision makes number fifteen since Christmas Day. I have experienced so much growth in my spiritual life through these visions and what I have been allowed to bring back to Earth. I can now say I am most definitely not the man I was seven days ago. Every day, the hours have increased. Time has slowed down. My mind is traveling at speeds unparalleled throughout my journey to date. Yesterday, I tried to discuss with Bryan the backlog of visions we have not talked about due to timing over the holidays (which was a backlog of twelve visions going into the phone call). We were not able to get through the whole list before he bailed on the conversation.

After the call, my mind hurt – not my spirit, not my heart, not my brain. My mind physically hurt. It was as if the visions I was sharing with him verbally were not being relayed spiritually to him. There was a disconnect. He was interactive in the

Rebirth II

conversation and seemed interested. He even asked me one question that resonated deep within me. His question: "How are you affected by the frequency of visions? Are you able to handle them? Are they affecting you negatively? When they increased for me, it was difficult – I just want to see how they affect you."

But, in response to his question, my answer was quite different than he expected. I explained that while the frequency of the visions for most would likely be teetering on the edge of insanity, I was not faltering in my walk. In fact, my understanding of the world around me was growing at such a fast clip, that it has caused time to slow down. I then compared the experience as tantamount to how, through the eyes of a child, every day is a day of learning. In a matter of a couple days or even a week, a child can be an entirely different person based on his rate of learning. I explained that a child may "have always Loved a certain food" or "always have known to do a certain action in response to a problem" though it would be readily apparent to the observer that the child had just acquired this new taste, knowledge or skill over the past few days. To a child, the days move slowly. Everything observed is stimulation and growth for the mind. As a human grows older, the rate of learning decreases relative to days lived. An older human is most certainly more knowledgeable and wiser than its younger counterpart, but the growth rate declines significantly in comparison to the number of days lived. I explained to Bryan I felt like a child – that every day right now is stimulating new growth in my mind.

The Written (cont'd)

Even upon our conversation ending and experiencing the sensation I felt in my mind, another avenue of understanding was unlocked to me. It is as if now I can understand how the architecture of my brain is evolving, growing, rewiring itself, creating new neural connections in response to my surroundings. The disconnect with Bryan was not for lack of communication — there is most certainly a spiritual obstacle in the way. But regardless of the cause, I experienced an (albeit painful) awareness of neural growth that rooted from our conversation. I also became aware that the knowledge and experiences I shared with him were perhaps too much for him to process with his current circumstances. It was almost like the feeling of my mind hurting was feedback — a response letting me know that I was forcing something into a place it did not need to go — like trying to make two dissonant notes sound beautiful together.

Whatever the case may be — and whatever the next steps are to come, the last week of these visions have been as a new day, a new life, a new understanding of All That Is. I have flashed in and out of multiple spiritual timelines that are now all becoming familiar to me. I am beginning to understand that the earthly experiences are intended to travel with my spirit to these other peoples and help them in some way — just as the experiences I learn from my visions are intended to travel back with me to Earth. I can tell I am interacting on a spiritual level, so I hesitate to say that these other places I am journeying to are anything other than parts of the heavens. There are always clear signatures for Divine locations in the heavens and interactions with spiritual elders. And though these visions seem to be different locales than each of those Divine locations, I can only surmise that these recent visions have brought me into more intimate terms with other levels of angels and spirits throughout the heavens unseen.

January 3, 2014
Early Morning

I was standing before a great angel who must have been ten feet tall. He began talking to me about different locations throughout the heavens. I was listening intently, though I felt somewhat lost in the conversation. It was as if he had been discussing the subject for a while, but I had just managed to tune in. I am pretty sure he noticed when my mind and spirit found harmony in the moment. He seemed entertained by me. He began talking about one city that held great importance. He must have recognized my disconnect in the conversation, because he stopped and asked, "Oh you haven't been there before?" A laugh bellowed from the depths of his stomach as his face lit up with a big smile.

He was a happy angel and had characteristics similar to depictions of Santa Clause (though he was distinctly different). I have seen him before, but our times together are sporadic. I responded to his question, "No – I don't believe I have." He said, "Well, you should visit sometime. It is kind of like Seattle. Have you been there?" I again said, "No." He said, "Well

The Written (cont'd)

then, let me show you what it looks like." He directed me to a table where a miniaturized model of a city rested on the tabletop. On the left side of the city (that must have indicated West in cardinality) was a giant spire. The spire dwarfed the city to its right. The city itself was divided into rectangular dimensions; I would again have to say that the width was approximately two and a half feet in the model, and the depth approximately one and a half feet. The city layout was perfectly rectangular. On the left side where the spire resided, the surrounding area was grass. The city itself contained skyscrapers and taller buildings made of alabaster. The buildings were aligned east to west. The major roads travelled north to south. If the rectangular plot of the city were divided into thirds, the left most third in the west was filled only with the spire centered on a platform within the surrounding grass. The remaining two-thirds on the right side was filled with buildings.

The angel continued to emphasize the spire to me. I studied it intently. At the top of the spire, was a circular landing, much like the spire in Seattle, WA. However, the spire was connected to a larger platform made of alabaster that stretched eastwardly, covering over two thirds of the city. I was intrigued. I could not figure out the architecture holding the structure in place. It was impressed upon me that inside the platform (which had windows along the outer walls) was another place that people visited frequently. I was thoroughly enthralled at the concept. I could imagine people walking into the base of the building and being taken up through the spire

Rebirth II

and into the building. The size was mind-bogglingly massive in comparison to the city.

As I studied it, the angel told me, "You should see it from this view." In an instant we were transported to the city where I was hovering above the spire. I could see straight down through the object. It was translucent, but I could still discern its architecture. Below, people were walking around the base of the spire and walking into it to travel up to the other level described to me. As I viewed the spire from above, I saw that the base of the ground beneath the spire was clear. It was as if the spire was built upon a large piece of glass. Beneath the glass, I could see blue sky and clouds. I asked the angel if it was really built upon something that was see-through. He said it was and asked me to keep studying it.

As I studied the base, I could tell the spire served as the center point of eight divisions. The outer lines that would normally connect the dividing lines to form an octagon were slightly concave. As I observed the design, I knew he wanted me to see the intricacies, but all of my senses were beginning to feel overloaded. I have to believe he perceived my mental struggle because we were transported back to the room. I was still standing before the model. As I studied the model, he asked me if I wanted to live above or below in the city. I was confused. I did not understand what he meant by above, since that portion was connected to the spire. He told me simply, "Look again."

I looked back at the model, and sure enough, above the landing was another level. I peered above the landing and ob-

The Written (cont'd)

served a second city overlaying the first. It seemed to carry a more elegant architecture, though it was tough to discern in the model. I continued to look above and then below, fascinated at the architecture. It was as if an entirely new city was revealed to me in a way that defies modern architecture. It was supported by the spire's building extension as well as two shafts on either corner of the right side of the base. As we continued to discuss the city and what was above versus below, I felt I was being told I currently reside below.

Suddenly, my alarm went off on Earth pulling my spirit out of the heavens and back to my body. I awoke. As I thought about the city, the spire, and the design, I could not help but feel as if I was being told metaphorically how multiple locales in the heavens exist compared to Earth. The concept echoed deep within me. The ratios and proportions of the city were equally important as they seemed to echo proportions mentioned throughout the Old and New Testaments in the Bible. I feel like the exercise in studying the city revealed many more intricacies about the heavens and the method of travel between the locales. I have so much more to learn, but this vision was definitely a lesson that deserves a great deal of introspection and further meditation.

Rebirth II

January 3, 2014
11:00 a.m.

I am definitely becoming stronger and more controlled in my astral body – though I have such a long way to go. I can now sense in the area around my third eye when there are opportune times for my spirit to travel. When Bryan and I originally began this adventure, neither of us initially thought much about the specific times in the day or night when our spirits would travel more easily. Over the last several years, the times in the night have become blatantly obvious and the times during the day are now beginning to come into view. In the recent few weeks, I have been acutely aware of a sensation above the roof of my mouth, behind my nose and through my forehead. This is a sensation I get during meditation and I am beginning to identify it now when I am not meditating. I identify it as my third eye. This sensation is almost like the spiritual side pinging you to see if you hear the call. While that is metaphorical, it does have a real-world meaning as well. I felt this same feeling today before I decided to meditate.

During meditation, I closed my eyes and began concentrating on thoughts outside of my mind. These thoughts seemed to morph from questions into an inner dialogue that eventually transitioned into a conversation with an angel as my spirit journeyed away from my body. I can only explain this by saying that the direction of thought distracts the mind enough during meditation that it allows the mind to stay focused on

The Written (cont'd)

the thought instead of the spiritual sensation of travel. It is sort of like telling a person who is afraid of heights not to look down. The action of looking straight ahead keeps the mind focused on something else while the body remains calm and collected in its action.

So as I meditated, I realized that I was standing face-to-face with a beautiful angelic female. She was talking to me so peacefully. She told me, "I am so proud of you and excited that you have learned to cross through the veil. Here relax. It is in the shoulders." When she said that my mind began racing as it identified its surroundings. This is often the most difficult part of finding spiritual harmony. She reached out and touched my shoulders and began massaging them. I felt every bit of feeling and sensation rush through my body. Her Love for me sent shockwaves through my soul. I began to lose harmony with the moment and I shouted out to her, "Hang on! I'm coming back! I lost you, but I'm still here. Don't leave. Hang on!"

The vision returned from the blackness into clarity. She was still standing before me, her hands on each of my shoulders. She said, "It is all in the shoulders. Don't think of two, think of one." This statement was confounding, but images were impressed upon me as she spoke those words. I saw a strap resting on each of her shoulders, and a strap resting on each of mine. The straps appeared to be part of the clothing we each wore and were deep green in color (almost black). I saw the image of each of her shoulders getting close to mine as she closed the gap between each of us. As she got closer, the

Rebirth II

straps on our shoulders ignited in a light-bloom as I saw her straps and my straps combine into one. As the image was echoing in my mind, I looked at her. She looked at me smiling, loving. We began to talk.

She continued to tell me about how excited she was I was passing freely through the veil and continued to emphasize how it was all in the shoulders (and to relax). During the conversation, I called her by name. Somehow, I knew her name. I repeated it several times throughout the conversation, each time impressing myself that there was actually a name spoken during the conversation. Eventually I began to lose my bearings at my excitement and my spirit came back to Earth. I immediately recounted the events over and over in my head to make sure I did not forget the moments. As I tried to repeat her name, I could not recall it in full. When I was speaking it in the heavens, it was difficult to say. When a word is difficult to say, it typically indicates that the word will be difficult to bring back with me. The only thing I can say with confidence is that her name contained the letter "M." Everything else would just be a guess or conjecture.

After I committed the vision to memory when I returned to my body, I tried once again to return to the heavens. This time, I was greeted in the heavens by two females. I never was fully able to bring myself into harmony with the moment. I imagine my window of opportunity was fading. I know we talked. We laughed. We spoke about the encounter I had just experienced and the brevity of the one I was having at that particular moment. But this vision faded nearly as quickly as it

The Written (cont'd)

began and my spirit returned to Earth. I knew that my opportune time for travel had passed, so I came back to journal the encounters.

January 3, 2014
5:30 p.m.

As I drove home, I once again began to feel that same sensation in my third eye. The sun was on the horizon, so this was becoming expected around this time. When I arrived home, I immediately sat in a chair so I could begin to meditate. My body went into a weightless feeling – common now during my meditations. However, my mind was still racing. I was acutely aware of all of the sensations, and my mind was thinking about every nuance. I began to refocus my thoughts on questions that I desired to be answered from the heavens. My mind flew through question after question, and it became obvious I needed to focus on just one simple thought. My mind returned to a question about the girl I have discussed recently. I had been praying for patience and strength as I had begun learning how to feel again. My question was not result driven – just a continual pleading for peace, because it was something I have struggled with. At best I hoped for some words of confidence.

My phone rang nearly pulling me out of the meditation, but I was able to refocus. I just kept repeating the question, "My Lord, will You please give me strength and help me find

Rebirth II

peace and understanding in how this will play out with her?" Perhaps the question was not the best question to ask, but it is the only one that would calm my mind. As I allowed my mind to focus on the question, the feeling of weightlessness became greater. I felt my spirit floating up, and suddenly I was washed in blue and white light. The sheets of light were flowing around me like you would imagine they would appear moving with a smooth, peaceful underwater current. I was mesmerized, locked into the moment. Suddenly, I became aware of a light whisper.

As I realized there was a voice whispering in the distance, I began to focus on it. Almost as quickly as I noticed the faint whisper, I heard a loud whisper in my right ear. In earthly terms, the whisper was nearly as loud and clear as someone speaking directly into the ear. There was no mistaking the whisper. The voice was spoken from a female voice. I feel confident it was the voice of "the girl" who recurs through my visits to the heavens. Her tone was loving, sweet, and spoken with an air of comfort. The words that were whispered were, "Keep biding the time. She will be with you." The last part of the words sounded somewhat garbled, but I think that was because I was almost in shock of hearing the words so clearly.

I guess I should be less startled by spiritual interactions like these – especially by this point in my journey – but it is still awe-inspiring when I hear the voice of a great angel speaking directly to me. As my senses captured everything in the moment – the words, the lights, the sheets flowing around me – I began to lose harmony in the moment. I continued to try to

The Written (cont'd)

focus, but I could tell that my question was answered, and the Divine conversation had ended. I opened my eyes still feeling the peace within my body. After a few minutes, I got up and walked over to my phone. The call I had missed was from my friend Lance. While I have not journaled much about it, his life has taken a strong turn for the better, and his journey is beginning to open up for him.

When I returned his call, he immediately wanted to offer me words of encouragement and strength with Lindsey. I have not spoken with him about anything with Lindsey in a week – and only then in passing, so it would have been a little odd that he would be calling to offer words of encouragement if it were not for my prayer that was occurring at the time of his call. All things are connected. Our lives are woven within an aetheric fabric of communication that the brain struggles to rationalize. At this point in my journaling, it should be clear that I have been completely transparent about my experiences, whether or not others choose to believe the words I have written. But this particular circumstance carries with it an extra level of truth. Even if I personally were not to believe or rationalize the words I heard spoken to me; even if I had not been mentally or spiritually aware enough to hear communication from the angels; the fact remains that while I prayed for words of encouragement and strength, my phone rang from a friend calling with that specific intention. Everything is connected.

Rebirth II

January 4, 2014

I am not sure how to even begin to describe the events from last night. It should be fairly obvious that over the last week the frequency and amplitude of my visions has been constantly increasing. This would prove to be the case last night as well. The strength of the visions was so grand that I fear the amount of words I will use to describe them will pale greatly in relation to their significance. Over the course of the night, my spirit was transported to the heavens no less than seven times. I continued to return to my earthly body and jot down notes as quickly as I could about each experience before attempting to journey back to the heavens. I can only describe last night as the equivalent of spending months, or perhaps years of earthly time in the heavens.

The first vision had me standing before an angel. This angel was asking for my help in accomplishing a number of tasks. Each time I was able to help her. Each time she became more impressed. The tasks did not seem significant (though I am sure there was more relevance than I took away from the moment). As my spirit gained a better grasp on its bearings in the heavens, I participated in a long conversation with the angel about my earthly experiences. I know there was specific mention about my location. I discussed with her the events of my last week of spiritual travel and that I was trying to learn whether I was journeying across timelines, locales, etc. She just smiled in response to my questions.

The Written (cont'd)

Eventually, another female angel entered the room. She stood before me and attempted to hand me a half-folded newspaper. I could tell there was a single bold headline spanning across the head of the paper and a picture that was large enough to bleed into the underside of the fold. I felt like the newspaper was a form of payment or reward for completing all of the earlier tasks. Each time the paper was extended to me, I waved my hands and said I would not take it. This occurred several times. In those moments, I did not think that the newspaper could have held answers to my questions about time and locale. But after returning to Earth to write about the encounter, I realized the error in my ways. In this case, trying to show humility was a flaw. Whereas, radiating humility is the proper expression of the trait. My effort to show humility prevented an obstacle in learning for me.

I returned to the heavens where I must have spent days being escorted around by a great male angel. He spoke to me about heavenly wonders and ancient knowledge. In all that I was told, I was only allowed to bring back a limited amount of information with me – partially due to me still learning what it is I am being taught, and partially because I have to assume that the information should be used as a whole and not in portions of completeness. The last part of our conversation was the most detailed and, of which, I was allowed to bring back in portion.

As the angel escorted me around, he took me to a Holy-of-Holies building within the heavens. Inside, there were numerous angels worshipping God. Many were praying. Some

Rebirth II

were helping others learn how to better tune their spirit. The angel and I were discussing the role of my spirit as being a bridge between the worlds. He spoke with an austere demeanor – clever, full of wisdom. I asked about how I would be able to use the spirit through me on Earth. I explained that if I can journey between the locales, then it would seem there was a way to manifest a bridge between the worlds. In point, I was not sure how to ask the question, because I was not asking for "special powers" per se, but I wanted to understand how to offer the spirit through me in order to serve God's will.

The angel told me there was much to learn and walked me over to a place in the room where I could witness others being taught some of the necessary knowledge. I watched as they learned how to pray. There were two specific motions made with the hands during prayer that were important in helping to manifest the bridge. One of the motions was in how a person is to hold the hands together and apart while asking for the Spirit to enter their body. The other motion demonstrated how to draw the Spirit out of the body and into the world. This motion was demonstrated by placing the hands in a 90° angle with each other while placing the thumbs together. The gap between the base thumb knuckles and the second thumb knuckles was to serve as the doorway. The hands were to be brought to the forehead where the doorway of the thumbs rested over the third eye. Words were to be spoken unto the Lord that helped manifest His Spirit. As the Spirit is to begin flowing through the doorway, the hands are to be drawn away from the forehead – as if pulling it out through

The Written (cont'd)

the third eye and into manifestation. I watched as each of the angels taught others this motion. There were other nuances in the execution of the motion and words, but what I have written is what I was allowed to bring back with me.

A third vision involved me speaking with angels about my earthly walk. I spent a long time discussing how I had grown on Earth as well as next steps for my journey. We talked for a while about Bryan and his journey. I told the angels how I was concerned that Bryan and I had a conversation recently and I felt like our spirits had some dissonance. They explained to me that Bryan was on his own path now. They explained that he had made remarkable changes in his life – some good, some bad – but overall, moving in the right direction. They emphasized he was about to be starting the respiratory program and that he would be spending a lot of his time working through those classes – but that he would succeed. They cautioned me not to pull him off of his path, emphasizing that my path was beginning to grow in a new direction from his. They also cautioned that he could feel stress for not having the same amount of visions that I was having recently, which could also serve as a distractor to him. Overall though, they sang his praises on his journey and accomplishments on the respiratory program.

The fourth vision involved the Rosalyn line. During my travels back to the heavens, I was taken to Europe where the Rosalyn line exists and has been popularized to be a marker within the Priory of Sion mythology. I have never seen it in real life – only once or twice discussed in documentaries about its potential significance. As the great angel escorted me

Rebirth II

around, he drew my attention to a rectangular plate. This indicated the Rosalyn line. There were no other markers – no other indicators that the line exists beyond this one rectangular plate. I could not discern its composition, though I would lean toward a discolored stone from its surroundings, or more likely a metal place within stone. The angel talked about its significance, but emphasized that what I was to learn and understand was the significance of its existence. The angel emphasized a time period of the 1300s when the line was created – though we did not discuss much more about the period in depth. While we observed the plate and discussed the line, a "child version" of someone important was present. Though I am sure the name was given to me, I continue to struggle bringing names back between the heavens and Earth. With the angel and me standing still, a couple showed up in the area, and cops arrived. I had to talk to the cops to keep them from the couple.

As we left the building, the angel took me to another location in the heavens. Again, I would have to guess that in earthly time, I was there for hours or days. He took me to a basketball court where we sat in the bleachers and continued our discussions. As we spoke, we watched an odd game of basketball taking place. I have to say it was odd because the players seemed completely out-of-sorts with their own physicality on the court. I watched as most of the players (kids and teenagers mostly) took long awkward strides and attempted half court shots throwing the ball clear over the basketball goal. It was a demonstration of amazing strength and awkward

The Written (cont'd)

coordination. It was almost comical in reflection – but I observed it as a place of training, so it did not seem funny at the time...just out of place. One young black girl whom I observed the most during my time there, was trying to make the team and continued to practice the awkward half-court shots.

Eventually the angel asked me if I wanted to try taking a few shots. I told him I did – that I played ball in high school and had missed playing. While on the court, I continued talking to the other players about all of the facts and numbers I had been told by my angelic teacher. We began playing a half court game of basketball. Every time the ball was thrown to me, I had a hard time figuring out how to dribble. The sensation of touch was not quite the same as it was on Earth, and gravity definitely had a different influence. Eventually, I figured out dribbling was more of a motion than a sensation, though I never quite mastered it. During the game, I took one shot at the goal and launched the ball clear over the backboard hitting the wall behind it. I must have over calculated the shot by a factor of two. When that happened I just laughed and said, "Well, I guess that's that." It seemed like some sort of a recognition and acceptance of my earthly basketball skills not translating over to basketball in the heavens. The game ended, and I returned to Earth to write about the encounter.

The next vision involved me being escorted by the male angel again. This time, the intention of the journey was for me to learn about science. I was walked into a room where I saw a prototype vehicle with a cage in the middle which seated one person. It was similar to the one from my previous vision that

Rebirth II

contained six large spheres along its base (in the shape of an earthmover). This time, I could see the vehicle had an oval base and was levitating off of the ground. I was told by the angel "Benjamin Hutton was able to do something significant because of Benjamin Leary's (or it could have been O'Leary's) invention." I was not sure if I was seeing the invention of Hutton or Leary, but my sense was that the invention belonged to Hutton.

As I observed the vehicle, the angel directed my attention to a dark-haired man with a darker complexion. I understood him to be of Eastern origin. The angel told me his name was Quam and that Quam's theories allowed everything that I was witnessing to happen. The angel then told me that "Quam was able to do it from Bekham and O'Brien." I have to assume that the angel was still talking about a specific scientific theory that began with Beckham and O'Brien, quantified and written about by Quam, which Leary and Hutton were able to use for this device I witnessed. There were so many names, numbers and theories being tossed around in that moment, that in trying to remember them all, I lost harmony and returned back to my earthly body. I tried to quickly research the names I was given when I returned to Earth – mostly finding references to theoretical physicists and quantum mechanics. I also ran across the term QAM – quantum wave modulation (which I suppose could also be what was being demonstrated to me through the vehicles levitation). I did not research too much, but I immediately prepared my body to travel back to the heavens.

The Written (cont'd)

While there are three more visions, I want to quickly write about the last one next because there is not as much detail to discuss and the final two I shall discuss are extremely significant. My last vision dealt with me sitting in an office. Before me was a document. Children continued to enter into my office to sign the paper. I would occasionally glance down and look at their signatures. After I decided to leave the office, I walked down a sidewalk and by a restaurant. I was walking with the male angel again. I decided to make reservations at the restaurant, so I stepped inside. Once inside, I talked with the staff about my day at the office, all of the successes that had occurred throughout the day, the number of emails I had received, etc. Once again, I was talking about much of the information I had learned throughout all of the previous visions and was talking like an expert in the fields. I can only imagine the other people I spoke to were unamused, but it was important for me to share everything I had learned.

While the last two visions I will discuss are not directly related to each other, they are indirectly related in a way that could only happen through the grand design of our Creator. The first vision I want to discuss turned out to be one portion of an answer to my prayer last evening. Even as it has become obvious throughout my journaling in how God continues to answer my prayers through visions, I am still amazed every time I hear His reply. It is quite possibly the most humbling experience that I could have. And while it is hard to quantify a scale of significance to heavenly encounters, I would have to

Rebirth II

say direct responses to prayers might be the grandest of all experiences.

In this particular case, I prayed for a friend of mine, Lance. As I have discussed throughout my writings, Lance has struggled with his walk and turned to me as a friend for help. But in the last few weeks, he has made a tremendous shift in directions for the better. Much of this has to do with a girl that has entered his life. It is the first girl that I have known him to talk about in the way he does. She clearly has given him hope that he could fall in Love once again – very similar to my recent experience as well. As he has gone through the weeks getting to know her, this weekend was the first weekend they will have seen each other in years. They have developed a strong relationship over the phone and through messages, but this weekend was going to be a big step for them. I prayed to God asking Him to grant Lance peace and strength in the relationship. I asked to keep his hopes and emotions in check, but to fill him with inspiration. What I did not expect, though, is the method that God would answer me.

I cannot even loosely begin to use any terms to describe the encounter in the heavens because all words fall short of any experience. Sometimes I use the word dream, sometimes vision, sometimes I talk about my spirit going to the heavens or to other locales. In all cases, it should be observed that the spirit is not bound to the earthly body. The earthly body hosts the spirit while we are conscious of our surroundings. But the spirit can transcend time and space – so to an outsider, there may be no other way to understand what I am saying describ-

The Written (cont'd)

ing other than through the use of the terms vision or dream. Another perhaps can understand the concept I am describing. But this time, the concept transcends the spirit just traveling to another locale or the heavens. My spirit traveled and met Lance's spirit and we had a conversation.

During the conversation, Lance shared with me all of the events of his night with the girl. He emphasized two firsts for him with her. These "firsts" were more in his description of feelings, but also in restraint of actions. He discussed how their kiss was different than most other kisses, yet that they only kissed during a much smaller window of time than would normally have happened with someone he liked. He talked about how they did not do anything beyond kiss, but he continued to talk about how turned on each of them were – and that his self-restraint was what kept the evening in check. For Lance, this was a big moment because it emphasized his feelings for her and his spiritual recognition in the moment. Between the "firsts" he experienced when they kissed and when they parted ways, I could tell he had a great evening with her. Regardless of where their journey will lead – I was only privy to talk with him about the events of the evening. This is where this vision ended.

Now while this might not sound significant, I decided to put the vision to the test today and talk with him about his evening with the girl. He echoed back everything nearly word-for-word as the conversation our spirits had the previous evening. While I did not share with him anything about the spiritual encounter, I just let him talk – careful not to bait him

Rebirth II

into any answers I hoped to hear. All that was emphasized to me was the reality of the spiritual experience I had encountered that evening with him.

So now knowing that not only was I having grand experiences in the heavens, but I was also spiritually jaunting about Earth and having late-night spirit conversations with my friends that proved out to be completely true, I can now say without a shadow of a doubt that this next vision continues to bring tears to my eyes every time I think about it. I shared the details of the experience with Bryan immediately following and even then, I could not stop myself from weeping. Out of all of the seven experiences in the heavens I had throughout that night and early morning, this experience was the grandest on all levels – its very essence permeating every emotion in my body.

As I have discussed here recently, my heart is being allowed to open up and experience Love again. Now as I write this, I want to emphasize that the word "Love" can be misconstrued through popular understanding of the word. The Love I am describing is a deep spiritual bond – a union of one spirit with another. It is a feeling that I am sure is identified with popular culture's definition of Love sometimes, but it is so much more significant. It is closer to a concept of agape. I feel it is necessary to define this because what I am about to write about could easily be chalked up to the definition of "puppy Love" or "lust" – neither being remotely correct. The Love I shall speak of is spiritual Love; purity; a blanket of all-encompassing warmth. And yes, it is most definitely possible to

The Written (cont'd)

feel this by proximity – much like a hand can feel warmth from a fire.

So with that said, it is important to understand that as my heart has opened up to the potential of Loving again on Earth, my body has raced with a swell of emotions. As I have written about it, my body has felt emotions erupting inside like a teenager may experience first Love or a first crush. This has all been part of reconditioning my spirit on my journey to once again be open. For so long since my divorce, my heart has been closed. This is the first time that I sense hope in an earthly Love in another is even possible. So that leads me to my prayer the last two nights. Over these two nights, my nerves have been on edge and my emotions racing inside in hopes that my relationship with Lindsey could develop into something grand. But the biggest part of this place on my journey is in the spiritual growth for potential. I do not want to sound over the top for someone that I have yet to get to know – I have not lost my understanding of the circumstances surrounding the situation. This is all about hope and potential from everything I do know about her. Anyway, my prayers about this part of my life have been a little different than usual. I asked for something I longed to experience, but have yet to do so at this date. That prayer, was to see her spiritually – to travel to her place and see her spirit.

I know on the surface, that may sound odd – but I have oft wondered how my spirit could interact with other spirits here on Earth. Even in my encounters with Bryan in the heavens, we were experiencing something together in a different

Rebirth II

time/space. This time, I just wanted to see her – to see her spirit; for my spirit to talk to hers and give her peace with her nerves. I can sense that she is nervous in meeting up since she has just gotten out of a long relationship. Perhaps the better term is guarded, rather than nervous. But in either case, she invited me to worship with her, and I have to carefully make sure that the spiritual walk is not encumbered by earthly desires. We have long had a good relationship that has been maintained at arms distance due to her last relationship, but now there is an impetus to build something closer, something under the guidance of His will. I understand it, even if I cannot properly put it all into words.

So, as I prayed, I hoped. I believed. I knew that God would allow this to happen if I was indeed ready and she was ready. So, now is where if everything else throughout my journals has seemed unbelievable, the next portion will exceed any likely hope at believability. For so it was that when my spirit mingled with Lance's earlier in the evening, the encounter was validated in tangible, earthly results. This time with Lindsey's spirit, the encounter would be the yang to the earlier encounter's yin. The encounter with Lance was placed in my experience so I could have tangible, earthly results to prove to my earthly brain that indeed everything is happening in reality and is being brought back to words as best as I can interpret the experiences. The encounter with Lindsey would be the unquantifiable – a spiritual encounter that cannot have justification in the earthly world.

The Written (cont'd)

As I have expressed before, one of the grandest experiences is to experience God's response to a prayer. In this case, I found myself in a room with "The Girl" (the female angel that continually appears with me in the heavens). I was sitting in a chair. She was asking me about Love. As I sat in the chair, there was a strange feeling from my chest through my neck. I could tell she was helping my spiritual body become conditioned for whatever was forthcoming. As she asked me about Love, I talked about it ad nauseum. The room was filled with such a warmth that all I could even feel was the feeling of Love. There was more Love experienced in this vision than almost any other spiritual experience I have encountered. It was as if she was turning up the amplitude to my feelings so that I would remember the moment. As the angel was listening to my answer, she turned away from me and faced something that required her attention.

Suddenly, I was standing in a room with Lindsey lying on the bed. The angel was with me as well. All I could do was stare. My mind was reeling at everything happening in the moment. The Girl asked me what I felt. All I could manage to say is, "I feel Love." I walked to the side of Lindsey's bed. Her body was illuminated from within. I saw her inner light glowing. She was beautiful. I was locked in her radiance. This is most definitely the first time I can say I recognized what I was seeing as a person's inner light. In earthly terms, it would appear almost like an x-ray image. Think of a transparent embodiment illuminated with a soft glow from within. I stared at her, soaking in every detail. She was lying on her left side

Rebirth II

facing away from me. As I studied her body, I recognized markings similar to that of a tattoo. I noticed other details upon her body. The space where the ink would have once been was illuminated similar to a scar – a defining edge on her skin. Since I had not seen her in so long, I was not sure if I was looking at the remnants of a removed tattoo or if it still existed. Seeing her in the form of her inner light was a little hard for me to understand at first as well, which probably made me unsure of how a tattoo would best be observed in this environment anyway.

Perhaps, the outline of the place of her old tattoo was just there to help me understand I was most definitely in the presence of Lindsey's spirit – something to serve as a name tag for me to recognize and differentiate her from others in the heavens. I continued to stare at her; I studied every inch of her body. The Girl asked me to look at Lindsey's back. I nudged Lindsey's right shoulder forward pushing her ever so slightly so that she would readjust, exposing her back to me. The Girl cautioned me to be gentle and to be careful.

For a moment, I had to understand two straps going down her back on either shoulder. Perhaps they were bra straps, but it was my impression I was observing the movable clasps and straps on a camisole. The difficulty in my understanding was because they were illuminated more densely than the rest of her body – in the same manner as the other markings upon her body. My earthly mind interpreted the markings and straps as tan lines, but again my mind was trying to understand and rationalize seeing a person's spirit illuminated

The Written (cont'd)

from their inner light. I guess it should also be noted that while I studied her body and I could see certain aspects of it, her body was shielded in a way from me so as not to tempt sexuality. Her spirit was pure and full of light, but clothed where it needed to be. The Girl asked me what I saw. I explained that I thought I was observing the straps to a camisole. She told me, "No. Not that. Look again."

I nudged Lindsey's right shoulder again and she stretched out onto her stomach, fully exposing her back. On her back I saw three scars that appeared like three lines next to the other, aligned vertically on her back. Each line was approximately 3 to 4 inches long – the middle one the longest. I stared, soaking it in. The Girl became quicker and more adamant with her questions. "What do you see?" I said, "I see hurt. I see pain. I see Love." She asked me again, "What do you see?" I again replied, "Hurt. Pain. These are scars. She is hurting right now. But I see Love." She asked me, "Could you Love someone like this?" Almost defensively I responded, "Yes. I can." She asked again. I responded, "Yes. I see her hurt. But I see Love." We flashed out of the room we were in back into the room from which we began the journey. I felt the same feeling I felt earlier around my neck as I sat in the chair.

The Girl looked at me again and asked, "What do you feel?" I again replied, "Love. Love! I feel Love." She looked at me and said, "Are you sure?" I again replied, "Yes." We flashed back into Lindsey's room. Not to say we repeated the exercise 100% identically, but it felt like a very similar experience. However, The Girl did not ask me as many questions.

Rebirth II

As I observed Lindsey and I witnessed the scars again, The Girl asked me one more time, "What do you feel? And are you sure you could Love someone like this?" To which I responded, "I see Love. And yes, I could Love someone like this." We flashed back out of Lindsey's room, and into the room from earlier. I struggled to keep my bearings and my spirit returned to my earthly body.

When I spoke with Bryan about it, he discussed with me his thoughts on the symbolism in the three scars. He thought that there was much for me to meditate upon with regard to the symbols in "The Stations of the Cross." Upon hearing my story, he felt immediately impressed to discuss the three falls that Jesus made while carrying his cross, and the symbolism in each one. While there is much to be gleaned, I feel strongly that Bryan has offered great truth upon the vision. While I did understand the scars to be figurative on Lindsey's back, I thought they represented pain that she has been through in her life with previous relationships. Bryan's assessment takes it several steps further to define it as the marking on a soul in a manner similar to the marking of Christ's soul. He felt that the marking could be symbolic to someone who is walking in Jesus' shoes and has suffered, hurt, and has carried pains and burdens with them during their time on Earth.

The analysis of the scars goes even deeper once the images and descriptions have been studied more in depth. I have to agree that the scars most definitely held greater meaning in the direction where Bryan felt led to interpret. I am still amazed in the experience; the answer; the emotion; the lesson; the Love.

The Written (cont'd)

Regardless of the identity of Lindsey being the subject of the experience, I know the greater lesson is in the construct and the concept of Love. As I am learning to feel again, it was important that the angels help me quickly grow in understanding spiritual Love. I am sure the heavenly lessons came with heightened frequency and amplitude due to how the rate in my earthly journey has increased. While I should emphasize that again, the lesson was on "Love," that in no way, shape, or form should be seen as an absolute with Lindsey – only the concept of the potential, and the spiritual understanding of the weight her soul has born throughout her time here on Earth.

January 6, 2014

Last night my earthly body was tired from the previous evening of only sleeping for an hour or two. During the previous night, my mind raced uncontrollably and my body continued to overheat. It was an exercise in frustration – like a child's mind the night before Christmas. Neither could I fall asleep, nor could I meditate and separate my body and spirit. It may have been the most frustrating night for me in the last several years. So, I could only expect that last night I would experience the opposite in that my earthly body would be too tired to separate from my spirit.

While I was partially correct with my body being tired, I did not have any problems separating my spirit from my body. The challenge was in finding harmony with the locales and the

Rebirth II

heavens. Whether it was intended for me to bring back information or not, I will not know. But last night was more of an exercise in spiritual travel. I managed to separate from my body on three separate occasions that I can recall clearly. Each time, I felt the motion of the great ocean of the Spirit take my body to another locale. There were interactions at each locale, but I felt that the purpose was to sharpen my ability to travel. After every interaction, I was sent on my way to the next location in the heavens. Indeed my earthly body was much more regulated in temperature than in previous attempts. I did not feel like I overheated at all throughout the night. But, I was able to travel about more freely. Morning broke, and my spirit was pulled back into my body.

It should also be noted that last night before I went to sleep, I spoke with Bryan for a long time about the previous visions I had experienced and the rate at which information was being relayed to me. The last time I spoke with him, I experienced a headache of great proportions afterwards. I understood that the headache was likely due to discussing certain content in the heavens that was intended to be for me only… sort of like a spiritual encryption from prying eyes and ears. This time I was much more careful in the conversation – but I told Bryan that I had to be careful about what I said. He acknowledged that he understood, but seemed confused on the matter. He pried for more information that applied to him and my conversations with the angels, but I simply danced around the subject.

The Written (cont'd)

After our conversation ended, I again experienced that abnormal headache from before. This time, though, it was more like a dull pain than an acute headache. I took this to mean that I again shared too much information, but I carried the conversation much better than I had previously. I was cautioned in my previous visions not to distract him from his course – that we were now going slightly different ways on each of our journeys. I suppose this is where the road diverges and "our journey" gains identities unto each of us. The journey is no longer "our journey," but rather his journey and my journey. We shared a common road together, and will forever be brothers in Christ – guideposts for each other along the way. The distinct methods and deliveries of God's word will now begin to take different shapes for each of us. I am not sure what the future holds for either of us, but I do know that we have reached a point of individuality on the journey. We are each able to understand the information being given to us without as much reliance on the other for interpretation. Where in the beginning, we each had to share our spiritual stories with each other – almost in justification that we were not losing our minds – we now each have the strength to carry forward on our individual journeys without the reliance on the other. Each person should trust that God communicates with him in a way that only he can understand. This moment is tantamount to the bridge from whence teaching a child to understand communication transcends into the moment a person realizes he is engaged in an adult conversation with that same child who only days before was still learning to communicate.

Rebirth II

January 8, 2014

During meditation, I had a brief vision where my spirit journeyed to another place. The angel standing before me knew I was not going to be able to hold harmony very long. He laughed when I appeared. He was leaning against the outside wall of a large building. The building best resembled a carwash, but I am not entirely confident that is what I was observing. There was also someone or something behind a closed garage door inside of the building. I understood that I was being held in line at a place to enter, but I was not confined by any rules keeping me in place, so I wandered around and over to the angel. He had (what appeared to) be a towel thrown across his shoulder. I had never seen him before. From this point on, I will refer to him as The Mechanic since that is how I perceived his role in the heavens.

As he leaned against the wall he pointed around to the line of vehicles and said, "I'll try to make it 153 and 259." He kind of smirked and smiled at me as if to say, "Yeah, he's not going to make it long enough here to make it through the line." I looked back at him. He said, "153 and 259 if you are lucky. That's if you are lucky. Good luck." I wandered back to my place in line, but lost harmony before I reached my destination.

Upon returning to my body, I immediately wrote down his words. While it may not be apparent from the description I have given, the numbers he gave me were a combination of

The Written (cont'd)

tones that contained a specific harmonic spacing within the earthly reproducible tones of the Pythagorean skein. The numbers should be thought of as two boundaries that intersect in the space of the eight-sphere, though I am still trying to learn its mechanics. These numbers were like a roadmap of sorts to return to a specific location.

January 11, 2014

Over the last several days I have had very weak visions, or the bizarre. I typically write a lot about what may seem like the insignificant to others, but often there is value to be found within. On the 9th, I did not experience anything. On the 10th, I experienced a setting I have visited before. It is the setting of an amphitheater where two performers entertained the audience. This is the second or third time I have found myself in the midst of a crowd watching the performers. Every time, the main performer sings a medley of songs, but the song that is continually the most vivid contains the first verse to "Friends In Low Places." It seems so oddly placed in my visions that I typically dismiss it and do not write about it. But I figure that since I have documented nearly everything else I have experienced, I will make an effort to document the bizarre as well.

The other thing that stood out in this vision was that both entertainers wore white shirts and baggy khaki pants. Their pants were rolled up about six or eight inches from the ground and they were not wearing shoes or socks. When they per-

Rebirth II

formed, they sat upon wooden stools and the main performer had his guitar with him. This had been the case each time I have found myself in this setting. This last time, the main performer made more jokes than typical and kept the crowd laughing. At one point, he climbed onto the edge of his stool and – in what can only be described as a gravity defying moment – extended his body parallel with the ground, balanced only by feet on the seat and first rung of the stool. There is zero chance that this would be possible on Earth which I suppose is why it stood out so vividly in the vision.

This morning, I realized I had experienced another night similar to the night I wrote about the ten visions. In the beginning of the visions, I was extremely tired and groggy. Due to the bizarre settings and surroundings of the visions, my mind initially tried to dismiss them as unimportant. The odd thing is that I had never really dismissed visions before. There have been a handful of bizarre settings that seemed to hold no importance, but even now I am making a concerted effort to keep track of those as well. But somehow over the last few days, the frequency of the visions has begun to cause my earthly mind to prioritize which ones to remember while attempting to maintain a deep sleep in the process. I also think this has to be due to the more strenuous workout routines I have put my body through recently, causing it to long to focus my energy on growth and restoration during slumber. This has to change, and I will be more proactive about this new turn of events now that I have become aware of the circumstances.

The Written (cont'd)

The visions last night spanned the course of at least several days – if not weeks. They were extremely vivid, but my body wrestled to maintain harmony. The settings were similar to others past. I found myself standing in a room with an angel. He knew me, though I struggled to recall his name. The room was empty. We were standing in the dining room of an upscale condo. The angel stood in the kitchen. A modern refrigerator was all that was defined from the wood cabinetry. The man had dark hair and a beard. He showed me around the condo as if I had not been there before even though it was very familiar. Though I did not live in it, I had visited it at least once before.

As our conversation evolved, I was able to understand it with a little more clarity. In the beginning, words were tough to discern. But as I listened and concentrated, the words became clear. The angel told me multiple times that it had been several days since they had seen me and were wondering where I had been. I told him that everything was good. I did not quite understand the context of the conversation as my earthly mind struggled to find harmony in the moment. As I tried to rationalize where I was and to whom I was talking, I asked the angel his name. He blurted out something unintelligible. For some reason I felt inclined to tell the angel why the condo was empty.

I explained to him that the previous tenant had just moved out. I told him his name and occupation. In this particular conversation, I mentioned earthly names of a tenant who had moved out recently from the condo I lived in. The

Rebirth II

angel looked at me confused. I could tell that I was blurring the realities and that he did not understand what I was talking about. I tried to explain a little more about why I thought the angelic tenant was the same as the earthly tenant from my blurred realities, but eventually decided to halt the justification. I knew I was just muddying up the waters.

After we got the conversation back on track, he invited me back for tomorrow to show his son around. I had to ask what his son's name was, even though it was embarrassing to me. He mumbled it a couple of times. It sounded like "Anthony." We wrapped up the conversation, and he emphasized that I should come back again tomorrow, and we parted ways. He left the condo and I followed shortly after. It should be important to note that I have been several days removed from any type of clear interactions in the heavens – so this interaction with the angel may have been to let me know that I should turn up the frequency of my attempts at traveling to the heavens.

When I walked out of the front door and into a common hallway, I saw another person I knew down the hall. He came up and greeted me and asked me how everything was going in my life. He asked if I had managed to get my finances in order. I was in an unusually happy spirit. I explained that I had finally gotten ahead of that hurdle and that I was now feeling like I was in a good place. I invited him into my condo unit which was just down the hall from where we stood. He hesitated. I was a little confused and said, "Have you not been in one of these before?" The man had a look on his face like I had

The Written (cont'd)

just offered him the opportunity to do something extremely rare and special. He just shook his head to tell me that he had not ever visited one of the rooms.

I opened my room and immediately picked up some bright red clothes on the floor. It looked like a red shirt, red pair of boxer briefs, and red socks. I walked up a couple of stairs and into what I can only describe as my bathroom, though it was unlike anything I have ever seen on Earth. I walked across the bathroom to a laundry hamper. It was stainless steel against stark white walls. I stepped back through the portal-type door and down the steps back into my room. He had not made it to my room yet.

I looked around the room. It was small – just big enough for me to live comfortably by myself. I had numerous musical instruments set up around the walls. I noticed several keyboards, an electronic drum set, and a couple other instruments I have no idea what they were. In the middle of the wall on my left was what I could only guess to be some type of sleeping system. Maybe it was a bunk bed. Maybe it was some other type of contraption. Again, it was unlike anything I have seen before on Earth. When the man came in, all he could do was comment about how nice it was. All I could think was that it was more cluttered than I would ever maintain anything on Earth. Regardless, we chatted just a few more minutes about the strides I had made in my earthly walk and parted ways. Somewhere shortly after, I lost harmony and returned to my body.

Rebirth II

After finding harmony again, I found myself again standing in the heavens. This place was unfamiliar though. Maybe it would be more appropriate to call it one of the in-between locations. Though I could not draw a map of the destinations, it does seem that there are places between the extremes that hold within them both good and evil. Those places can be particularly scary and are oft explained as nightmares to those who are unfamiliar with the territory or their own spiritual walk. These are the places that the spirit must first understand during rebirth, though they continue to recur throughout the journey.

In this case, I was wandering around a large, abandoned factory. The setting was dark and had a damp feeling. I walked down a series of steps looking for a bathroom. It seemed I was on a quest to find the locker room where workers showered and changed clothes after work. I imagine that is where I guessed the bathroom would likely be.

As I wandered around the building I saw a few lost spirits. They seemed harmless, but they still evoked uneasy feelings. When I reached the bottom of the stairs, I walked into the locker room and into the bathroom. Out of the corner of my eye I noticed two men being intimate with each other. I could tell they were surprised and shocked that anyone else would be in the locker room. I rounded the corner to go to the bathroom, and I knew that trouble was about to ensue. Instead of using the restroom, I just stood there and waited.

I knew these two men were angry that I had witnessed them together and were going to come try to start something

The Written (cont'd)

with me. In that moment I felt anxious, yet strong. The men came in and began shouting at me, threatening me not to tell anyone. Even though I planned on not telling anyone, I could tell they were not going to let me out without a fight. I looked within myself for strength. As I found a great strength within, I envisioned my body growing to great proportions. In the last several trips to the heavens I have experienced my spirit in a size larger than others. I assumed it must also be relative to spiritual strength, so I envisioned my body growing in size. My intention was to grow and erupt into a giant burst of energy that blew them away from the surrounding area. I envisioned the strength of my spirit metaphorically parting the waters around me, creating a burst of protection that would blow back those in proximity by force. It is important to understand at this point that my spirit was clearly not on Earth as we define it. My spirit was in another dimension/realm/heavens/etc. My body remained on Earth, but my soul had journeyed elsewhere.

To date, I have had an inordinate number of electromagnetic interactions that I have initially dismissed, but have had to take notice as the frequency has increased. Cell phones drain at rates much faster on my body than on another. This has been tested and verified. Other electronics will receive power surges during my use and become irreparable. During one of my first practices with understanding my Qi during a deep meditation, I managed to cause a building power surge. Some of these occurrences have been documented. Some of them have not. But it is important to note that even I can no

Rebirth II

longer dismiss the inordinate number of electronic malfunctions in my presence.

So, what happened next in this vision is one that continues to reverberate in my mind. As I envisioned this burst of energy around me as my spirit grew in size and protection, my spirit let out every bit of energy that I desired to release. In this experience in the heavens, I properly executed this burst of energy. But – upon the release of the energy, my spirit was flung back in great force to my body on Earth. At this exact moment there was a brilliant flash of lightning in the sky and roar of thunder on Earth. My eyes were wide-awake. I had not hallucinated the lightning or thunder. It was real. And at that moment, a sudden burst of rain fell from the sky. I remained awake for quite some time hearing the roll of that single burst of thunder fade into the distance while waiting for more lightning and/or thunder. None was to be had. The rains ceased and the storm went away.

Now I cannot tell you if I somehow managed to manifest a storm or manifest the lightning or thunder, but I have a hard time rationalizing science over spirit in this case. Also, I suppose it could perhaps be viewed as the atmosphere was in an ideally charged state when my spirit made a call for a burst of energy, thereby allowing the skies to echo back in the form of a bolt of lightning and thunder. Whatever the case may be, I have been experiencing an increasing number of the inexplicable in my journeys to the heavens. Even if the stories in the beginning seemed fantastical, it seems almost absurd to say I created a lightning strike and burst of thunder – but I can tell

The Written (cont'd)

you with a straight face and with every ounce of belief in my body that I did. I may not understand all of the mechanics well enough yet, but that bolt of lightning and thunder were the product of my spiritual actions in that moment.

The final vision involved Lindsey. As it has been obvious over the last several weeks of journaling, I have been facing an internal struggle with the strength I need to keep faith in meeting up with Lindsey. Though I will be short on some of the details in this journal entry, it is important to understand that I picked up a bookmark to give Lindsey when I see her at church on Sunday. The bookmark holds much more significance in so many ways than just the concept of a bookmark, but that is for another time. For now, just understand that it is extremely important she receive this bookmark.

So as my vision began, I found myself sitting in church with my daughter. The service ended, and she and I headed toward my car to leave. When we had almost reached the car, I suddenly remembered I did not give Lindsey the bookmark. Then, nearly as suddenly, I realized that she was not in the service. There was a series of disheveling thoughts that seemed like a circus of confusion in the vision. It was at that point I realized that the vision was telling me that Lindsey would not be at the service on Sunday – though she had invited us. In the midst of the turmoil and confusion, I lost harmony and returned to Earth.

Update: Even though Lindsey had invited us to the service, she did not show up "due to a surprise out of town guest arriving."

Rebirth II

January 12, 2014
Day Notes

Lance invited me out tonight for dinner. He is not going to be in town for a couple of weeks and wanted to catch up on everything with Lindsey. He knew I had been having a hard time working through how the events have played out with meeting up with her. We met at a restaurant down the road from me – his choice. Ironically, it was the same place Lindsey and I had first met. When we entered, the restaurant was filled with people. There were no tables or even seats at the bar to have dinner.

We walked around the room, looking for seats. We stood at the corner of the bar when I took a step forward to grab menus. As I did, a man at the end of the bar stood up and darted out of the room. The girl (who I thought was his girlfriend or wife) made some weird motions, stood up, looked at me, looked at Lance, ducked her head and scurried out of the room. Lance looked at me and said, "That was weird."

As we sat down and ordered, Lance kept trying to give me advice on Lindsey. I eventually looked at him and said, "I know it is not going to make a lot of sense right now, but just know that there are three trials I must face with her." He had no idea what to say. Spiritual talk is minimal at best between us. He asked me to explain. I told him that while I would not be able to put it all into words, for him to know that in the last several years of my journey I had found a close relationship

The Written (cont'd)

with God. I told him in brevity that God communicates with me in a way He trusts I can understand and has communicated to me that the circumstances with Lindsey have a purpose in my life.

As we chatted, we were about half way through our dinner when the entire bar cleared out – as in 100% of the people in the room. I looked at the bartender and asked if that was normal. I knew what had happened, but I wanted Lance to hear the words she would say. She looked at us and said, "No. That was weird. It usually slows down, but I don't know what just happened." As Lance and I sat there finishing our dinner, he shared with me some spiritual stories in his past. This was the first time he had shared anything religious with me. It was a great moment for us. After he finished, I told him I no longer enjoy going out to restaurants or bars because "this happens."

I pointed at the empty bar. I explained that Bryan and I had been making jokes about it over the last couple of years. Though I did not talk about it in depth, I just let him think about what I had said. In truth, the stronger my spirit has grown, the more recognition others on Earth have of the spirit and subconsciously choose to leave when in circumstances that invite darkness (such as drinking at a bar). It is like how an old western movie portrays a bar clearing out when a known outlaw walks in. Words are not spoken. People just react in recognition of spirit.

As Lance soaked in what was going on, I could tell he was wrestling with the potential. Suddenly, a girl whom Lance had once been interested in dating appeared from nowhere,

Rebirth II

grabbed his arm and said, "Good to see you again." And, just like that, she walked out the door. Lance looked at me and said, "Okay. Now everything is weird. When we sat down, the couple acted strange when you got near them. The bar cleared. And now, she appeared from nowhere. She didn't have to come up to me or talk to me. I didn't even see her." I just nodded my head and we finished dinner.

At the end of dinner Lance said, "Let's go somewhere else and see if you can do it again." I told him that is not how it works, but since I was enjoying our conversation I told him we could go somewhere else if he wanted….but to not expect to see this happen again. We entered another restaurant down the road. There was only one seat available at the bar. A beautiful blonde was sitting in the seat next to it with her boyfriend next to her. Lance looked at me and said, "Why don't you sit down there and see if the bar will clear out so I can have a seat?" He was saying it sarcastically, but as I took a few steps toward the chair, the couple turned around and ran off. Literally. They ran.

Again, it was similar to the situation to the first experience. Cash was dropped on the table without a bill and the couple ran off. Lance looked at me and just said, "Okay. Now this is really weird." I told him, "Again, don't expect this. Just trust that what I said is true, and you will see it happen over time." We did not order anything. He wanted to go somewhere else. He was intrigued. We walked in and out of the next place he chose – again not ordering anything. This time I made no effort to walk toward the bar. In all that I was ex-

The Written (cont'd)

plaining to Lance, I emphasized that it was not a demonstration of showmanship. I just wanted him to know that there were reasons why I no longer went out all of the time.

As we circled through the last place, a girl was blocking the path to our exit. She was dancing – in her own world. I tried three different times to walk around her, each time I was met with her obstinacy to move. Eventually, I touched my hand on her back and said, "Excuse me." I walked on knowing what Lance would witness. When we each got outside, he looked at me and said, "Dude. What did you do? What did you say?! She completely stopped what she was doing and gave you a look like you just ruined her night. It was weird." I told him simply, "Just understand in what you witnessed by my presence, is only that much more powerful in touch." He stood there soaking it in. At that point he decided that he did not need to see anything else. He believed. We walked to the car, and he dropped me back off at my place. He told me how he wished he had a better relationship with God and was envious of where I had gotten – not in what he witnessed, but in my understanding and communication with Our Creator. We talked a little longer before I got out of the car. It was a blessed evening.

Rebirth II

January 15, 2014
Early Morning

Last night I experienced another several month long journey into the heavens. When my spirit returned to my body and I awoke, I decided I would wait a few minutes and write it all down when my alarm went off. I figured that it must be close to morning due to the duration of the vision. It turned out I was wrong, and I probably had another several hours before my alarm would eventually go off. During this time, my memory became hazier about the details.

This is the importance of writing down everything as soon as it occurs – or at least not allowing sleep to separate a vision from writing it down. The brain must stay active to recall the events in clarity. With that said, the experience found "the girl" and me in the heavens. She took me around many places – all glorious in awe and wonder. There were beaches. There were mountains. There were beautiful cityscapes. While we walked around, she continued to talk to me in ways in which I could interact at the time – though I cannot recall in clarity any of the details of her words.

The journey was exciting. I felt as if she was showing me parts of my life that were to unfold. The whole experience left me feeling that I had a glimpse into my future timeline on Earth and what I was to do during that time. We spoke of relationships, Love, life. When this portion of the journey ended, I was left feeling satisfied and excited about what was to come.

The Written (cont'd)

Near the end of the experience, I fought with maintaining harmony in the moment. Eventually after losing it and returning, I found myself in an unfamiliar place. It felt like the in-between-world I have spoken of before.

I wandered through a wooded countryside and arrived at a house. I knew the house was not mine, but it belonged to someone close to me – perhaps a family member or relative. As I walked around the house looking for any sense of life, I knew I needed to be inside. I could not tell you why, except that the house served as protection from an uneasy feeling I had standing outside on its grounds. In fact, the whole time I was searching for the house, my quest was driven by the desire to find safety.

When I walked around the back of the house, I saw a sign leaning against a rear wall of the house that said something to the effect of "This is not your house." I walked to the back door and turned the knob – it was unlocked. As soon as this happened a man appeared, cresting over a hill behind the house. He shouted out, "Hey!" He looked as if he lived off the land, and I felt threatened by him. I knew the house was not his. He was more like a parasite.

I turned to him. He was pointing at the sign leaning against the house in a way that indicated he was never allowed into the house, and I should not either. He was both in shock that I had opened the door and also envious. He wanted to follow me in. I did not let the man get close. When he was about twenty yards away I shouted, "Get out of here. This is

Rebirth II

my house." I felt my spirit grow large. The man cowered and ran off into the distance.

When I walked inside I could tell someone else was in the house. With each step I took, I heard someone rustling into another part of the house away from me. The kitchen had a warm cup of tea on the table, still steaming. In the living room, the television was on – as if someone had just been in there. I shouted out, "Hello! Is anyone home?"

As I wandered through the house, I continued to shout out those words. When I reached the front sunroom, I saw a figure outside of the window. It was a brunette girl. She walked to the front door and opened it. She was svelte and pretty. She was taller than me, indicating her spiritual presence. She looked at me lovingly and said, "That was cute. How you said, 'is anyone home?'" She found my words funny – as if I was making wordplay on being home in the heavens. I just snickered and said, "Hi." I asked her who she was. She looked at me with powerful eyes and said, "Oh – we've met before. I'm Erin/Aaron."

Now – here is where I have to clarify her introduction. As she began to say her name, my mind tried to rush to finish the answer. The word I thought she was going to say was "Erin" because she resembled a girl I once knew named Erin. She had distinct facial features (a mark on her forehead) that made me keep thinking of that name while I stared at her. However – as she finished saying her name, my mind sort of blocked out the ending of her words as it raced in thought about the chances of an angel looking like someone I knew on Earth. It is

The Written (cont'd)

possible that perhaps it was the angel Arielle – though I do not think that is the case. It is possible that it parallels to the Aaron mentioned in the book of Numbers in the Bible, for Aaron had an explicit name written upon his forehead. I hesitate to say one or the other with complete affirmation, though I do know I was standing in the presence of a great angel. As all of the thoughts raced through my mind, I lost harmony and returned to my earthly body.

January 15, 2014
Afternoon

During meditation today, I was given an image. It was the Star of David bound by a circle smaller than the outermost edges of its points. Along the edges of the circle was an array of triangles that wrapped around it like a sun. The centermost triangle on the Star of David was nested in the top most triangle of the sun. The triangles on either side of the center triangle were equally as large and covered the perimeter to the edges of the Star of David's top outermost tips. The other triangles were arrayed around the bottom for a total of nine triangles surrounding the circle.

January 16, 2014
Conversation with Bryan

Bryan shared with me a conversation tonight about an event that happened to him earlier in the week. He did not

Rebirth II

know why he felt the reason to tell me, but he knew it was important. As he was driving, two cars came around a curve clearly about to hit him. He took his hands off of the wheel and – in what he could only describe as an instinct he had never felt before – made a motion with his hand in the direction of the cars. His hand was in a form similar to something you would see in martial arts, but only similar – not anything like he has ever done before.

Upon him making the motion, both cars came to a lurching stop before him. He had no idea where the motion came from, where the instinct came from, or even what really just happened. He just was a vessel in a moment for God. As he shared this with me, my eyes welled up in recognition of some of the events that have been happening in my life. Though I did not share the lightning strike with him or anything else of recent times, I knew that his words held God's handshake with my soul in those moments – letting me know that what I think I have been experiencing is indeed very real.

January 16, 2014
Early Morning

Last night was a night filled with visions. I did not feel well earlier in the evening and decided to skip my daily workout and allow my body time to rest. I went to bed extremely early, though I was not very tired. I had recently taken notice of a sensation in my nasal cavity that queues me into the precise

The Written (cont'd)

moment my body and spirit separate. It creates a tingly feeling in my nasal cavity and the top-back of my throat creating a pressure from that point to my third eye. I am not sure if I could say I have control over it, but I do have an acute awareness. It provides me with a dual recognition of my body and spirit. Most spiritual experiences are not as extreme as the ones that jolt me into recognition in the midst of meditation or sleep, but they are very vivid regardless.

As I lay down, I became almost instantly aware of the vibrations in my body. I knew it would be a night filled with visions. Almost immediately upon shutting my eyes, I found myself sitting before a king and queen. The queen was looking at me as if I was a child – perhaps a baby. She said, "Meet King Henry, II." I am not sure if I was experiencing a moment where I was the person being introduced as King Henry II or if the man before me was King Henry II. Whatever the case, my mind raced. I knew I had just shut my eyes, and this was, by far, the most random experience I have had. My spirit returned to my body. I felt like my spirit was traveling through the archives of the akashic records and that this experience was just randomly one I happened to experience upon shutting my eyes. I rolled over to journal the moment. From the time I had climbed in bed to this point, six minutes had passed. Within those six minutes, I had also said a long prayer before bed. All I can assume is that as soon as I shut my eyes and allowed my breath to settle, my spirit launched into the heavens.

Rebirth II

Nearly as instantly as the first experience occurred, I had my second experience of the night. After journaling, I closed my eyes and settled my breath. Suddenly I was in a version of my condo that I live in currently. I walked into my bathroom which contains a large walk in closet. As I stood in the closet hanging up a coat, a girl came in and handed me an overly large coat. She tried to hang it up but did not put much effort into it. The coat was large enough to pin me under it as she tried to hang it. The inside was like satin. However the outside had thick, furry sleeves. I was extremely confused as to (a) who she was, (b) why the coat was so disturbingly large, (c) what was suddenly going on in my condo, and (d) how to get out from underneath the coat.

I eventually managed to slide out from underneath the behemoth of a coat. She rattled off about the coat, its qualities, and why she brought it to me. I was puzzled. All I could think to say was, "I don't think this is what I wanted…." She did not seem upset about my answer – more like my answer did not matter to her. She brought me the coat, and that was her purpose. The girl had short pink hair. She wore a white t-shirt and short shorts. Her shoes were similar to the converse style "skater-chick" would wear on Earth. She also had white suspenders. She was clearly operating to the beat of her own drummer.

When she finished telling me about the coat, she turned and pranced out of the room. Just as suddenly as she left several other people pushed their way in, followed by a man larger than the others. He wore a slick blue suit. His hair was

The Written (cont'd)

dark brown and slicked back. He was slender, but athletically built, and I could tell he enjoyed living a flashy lifestyle. He wore a pair of glasses that I understood was for style and not out of necessity. They were round and had pink lenses. He had a mustache and a beard and carried a straight cane (though again, it was not out of necessity).

I was immediately uncomfortable in the moment. I sensed evil. He was very flamboyant in his mannerisms as well. His intention in entering the room was to talk to me, and I wanted nothing to do with him. I honestly believe I was staring at either Lucifer or Abraxas face-to-face. They both have appeared in visions of Bryan's and mine before, but only once had the entity identified himself as Abraxas to Bryan. So, whomever the entity was, it was most definitely intent on derailing the train I had boarded on my journey with God. The man turned to me and made a sinister motion with his fingers. He said, "I don't think she is the one for you." I knew he was talking about Lindsey and not the girl that had just left. I pushed my way through the room and out the door. I summoned my spirit to return to my body – I needed to jettison from that experience of evil. I awoke and journaled about it.

The night continued to be a test of my spiritual strength. It was a type of night that I have rarely had. By the second vision that I had just experienced, I knew that my conversation with Bryan earlier in the evening had been heard throughout the heavens and had attracted those wanting to derail me from the strength I had found in my recognition of this part of the journey.

Rebirth II

In the third vision, I was at a house having what I can only describe as a spiritual bonding with others inside. The house represented strength and protection. It became time for me to depart and I got in my vehicle to drive away. I left the house and drove through the neighborhood. I sensed danger. As I drove, I became lost and eventually had to backtrack. As I crested a hill, I saw flashing police lights at the base of the hill. I saw a girl lying down on the ground, hands behind her back being arrested. I knew that she was a good spirit, but for some reason the security was out in force to remove the good people from the neighborhood. I knew I would have to drive through them, and I would be arrested.

When I reached the base of the hill, they asked me to get out of the car. They ran my credentials and told me I would have to stay with them. They took me to a jail – though I never felt like I was being arrested. I was put in a holding cell with a very unattractive, butch girl. I was told that "she wanted me to know what it was like to suffer."

I sat in the cell with her and observed a large community cell before us. In the rafters were strange, inverted T-shaped contraptions. They were stacked upon each other similar to how efficient hangers and tie racks allow more than one shirt to be hung in the space of one hanger. But there were no more than four of these T-bars in a stack. I observed as the group of female inmates standing beneath the T-bars climbed into the rafters and inverted themselves like bats hanging on the T-bars. This was how they slept, how they relaxed. Some T-bars stood apart from the others, but most were stacked, causing

The Written (cont'd)

the rafters to become filled with bodies of those who were suffering. The inmates also seemed to be eating each other's flesh and exhibited a disgusting and uncomfortable sexuality in their actions, though that is only a very basic explanation of what I witnessed. Eventually, I was allowed to leave, and I walked outside of the prison building. I knew I was supposed to see the filthy moment with the T-bars for a reason, and that I was not "arrested" for any other reason than to witness that situation. My mind wrestled with the thoughts. The walk still felt unsafe, and I was uneasy in the setting. I returned to my earthly body.

The last vision of the night involved another negative energy and temptation. I found myself sitting among a group of people. The person leading the group was instructing everyone to pair off. The girl to my left was attractive. She was brunette and slender. She had distinct moles or markings on her body that differentiated her from the usually pure forms I see in the heavens. She was dressed in a slinky white shirt that was very flattering, but revealing. She looked at me and said, "I'll have sex with you." Having no idea what I was even doing in the situation, I looked at her and said, "You will? Awesome." Then I high-fived her. Our hands did not release from the high-five. We held hands while the instructor continued talking. When he finished speaking, everyone had coupled up and left the room.

We were left sitting upon a mattress. She immediately jumped into my arms and began kissing me. I was still trying to digest what was going on because I knew that my heavenly

Rebirth II

walk would not have this type of situation happen without a purpose. I returned the kiss and pulled back. I said, "Don't we need to go somewhere?" She just smiled and said, "No. I want it right here." She wrapped her legs around me and pulled me on top of her. Her shirt slid around her sides revealing her breasts and stomach. She pulled me in to kiss her more. The kiss only lasted the briefest of seconds as I finally gathered my bearings and thoughts. I backed off and sat straight up. Trying to come up with any words I could to prevent the situation from happening, I told her, "Listen. Before we do anything, I need you to know that I can't do this. I really like a girl whom you know, and I cannot do anything that would hurt her." She looked at me both broken-hearted and confused. She immediately ran off.

    I sat on the bed mulling over the events that had taken place. I felt guilty for even kissing the girl, but at the same time I knew there was nothing I could do to prevent it because I had not rationalized the spiritual test quickly enough to stop participating before we even paired off. My heart was heavy. As I sat there, the girl came back in and sat down beside me. This time, she was larger in size which helped me understand that she was an angel in disguise.

    She sat down holding her knees in her arms, her barefoot feet fidgeting with each other in those moments. She asked, "So you really like her?" I said I did. She continued asking me about her and about why I stopped doing things in the moment with her. She seemed hurt. She asked why I would not "do something" when the girl I liked was not even around. She

The Written (cont'd)

did not leave me any room to answer between her questions, as they seemed more like a stream-of-consciousness thought process. When she paused, I told her, "Because some things are worth waiting for – and she is worth the wait." The girl then began to reveal her true identity, stripping away the disguise she wore. She was indeed an angelic being sent to test me.

She asked me a couple of questions about who the girl was even though her questions indicated that she already knew it was Lindsey, but did not want to ask me directly. She eventually said, "Can I ask – is she named Lindsey?" I nodded. She said, "That is who I thought it was. She is dating someone else – (insert a name I cannot remember) – just so you know." She also imparted an image of the guy to me with a goofy hairstyle by any standard. The angel turned to leave. I told her, "That doesn't matter to me. She is worth waiting for. Please don't tell her. Please don't let her know you know about me. I want it to work, but she can't know about my feelings yet. I don't want to scare her off."

The angel vanished into the distance. My spirit returned to my body. Was the angel good or evil? I do not know. Was the angel sent to test my faith, or add doubt? Again, I do not know. Was her telling me about Lindsey dating someone a truth or a lie, a way to add doubt or a way to test faith? Was the image of the guy to give me confidence in my own appearance, or to introduce doubt? Again, I do not know. Perhaps it is all of the above – for the only thing that could possibly have

Rebirth II

been introduced to me was "fear" – and that part of my walk is unwavering.

January 17, 2014

 The events of yesterday evening played into a series of events and visions that I had early this morning. So before getting into the visions, it is important to understand that Lindsey and I were texting again last night. This week when we have texted it has lasted for several hours straight before turning in for bed. Responses were quick and we have both been attentive. The texts have really been warming her up to me and helping her see again. So after a series of funny texts yesterday afternoon, we began our routine of nightly texts.

 Right as that routine started, I had a knock at my door. It was Jason. I thought Jason was returning a movie he borrowed – and indeed he was – but, he wanted to linger. Jason and I have had a really rough friendship for the past several years, and I know he is trying to rebuild it. I have been open to rebuilding for years – but he has had a hard time getting over an event that seemingly changed his life for the better, but is mad because it was not under his control. Anyway, I digress.

 So, when he was in my place, he wanted to tell me about his upcoming wedding and the ring he is buying. I knew that Lindsey was texting me during this time, but I am honestly one of the worst at multitasking when it comes to personal attention. Texts fall by the wayside during conversation, and

The Written (cont'd)

conversations suffer if I am texting. In an effort to hurry Jason along and devote all of my time to texting Lindsey, I had to ride out the awkward duration. He stood just inside my doorway for about thirty minutes. It was obvious he was not staying, but also obvious he was trying hard to talk to me. Eventually it ran its course, and he left.

I looked at my texts only to discover that Jason's visit might have been one of the most ill timed visits I have experienced. Lindsey had one of the worst days of her life and was pouring herself out to me. She even put the crying face at the end, apologizing for dumping all of that on me (after I had not responded). I am sure my delay in responding seemed like an eternity and a cold shoulder to her opening up to me. Quite possibly this was the worst thing that could have happened. If we were on phone-call terms yet, I would have picked up the phone and called, but since she seemed to be keeping somewhat of an arm's distance in protection, I immediately replied back apologizing for the delay explaining my neighbor had an ill-timed visit.

In my haste, I did not write the most suave reply, but I thought it was as best as I could recover for looking like a jerk when she started opening up to me. Keep in mind she is fragile from her breakup. My text went unanswered for about an hour – so I texted a question back at the end to gauge whether she was upset at my absence or perhaps on a phone call herself and could not text. No reply…all night. So – there is that. I clearly had found myself in the middle of a frustrating moment in her eyes…and rightly so.

Rebirth II

So, I thought long and hard about a recovery today....a recovery for someone who I had not spoken to on the phone yet or seen in person in three and a half years. This is quite possibly one of the strangest challenges I have had because I know she likes me, and I her. I had to reach deep within to understand that in my frustration at the events, there must be a purpose and a reason – somehow Jason coming over at that specific time was intended...maybe by the devil (hence my vision from the previous night), though God is my all. He is my King. I know that he allowed this obstacle to be placed in my life for me to overcome.

I decided my best course of action was to go to a local hand-made chocolate shop in town and order their one pound gift boxes for each of the staff where Lindsey works and have them anonymously delivered. After I had given them time to enjoy the chocolate, I planned to text her the following message:

"I hope you and your coworkers enjoyed what I sent over this morning. I know you were pouring out a lot to me last night, and I can't imagine being told what you had to hear from your boss. I know the timing couldn't have been worse with my neighbor & I apologize for that. Also, after rereading my response, I'd give it maybe only a C- at best too...so there's that as well. Anyway – please know, I hope you have a better day today :)"

But – seeing as I sometimes jump to grand gestures too quickly in my candor and generous heart, I did not know if that was the right step. I prayed for guidance from my King. I apologized for my challenges I was having in strength and

The Written (cont'd)

asked Him to fill my body with support. As I struggled to fall asleep, I worked on rewriting that draft text over-and-over until I thought it sounded right. It was only then that I tried to fall asleep.

Even after finishing my draft, I lay awake for hours – unable to fall asleep. I came to realize I was afraid to fall asleep, which was a first for me. In light of the spiritual experiences from the previous night, I really did not want to see Lucifer again. I knew he could not hurt me, but until you stare at the devil face-to-face, it is hard to put that feeling into words. Bryan and I have each seen him at other points in our journeys (in various disguises) and every time we are left with a haunting feeling. Perhaps, he was the reason behind Jason coming over – trying to rattle my mind. Who knows...? Anyway, I decided to text Bryan in the wee hours of the morning and tell him about the fear. I did not expect a response because I was sure he was sleeping. My text to him only mentioned that I had seen Lucifer the previous night, and that I found myself struggling to fall asleep for fear of seeing him again.

Eventually I was able to fall asleep. There was an odd in-between state that occurred as I meditated to still my body. In that state my spirit passed through a realm (past/future/etc.) where I heard conversations from other people about soccer games and other random material. Eventually, my spirit found itself in a great vision provided by God to help me understand the situation I was experiencing.

My spirit was on an incredible yacht. This yacht was extremely large – like a cruise ship. It was very luxurious and

Rebirth II

had just returned from successfully chartering a large group of people. The captain stayed in my focus the entire time. It was important I witnessed the events as he experienced them. The passengers wandered around on the boat and began leaving. Their conversations discussed the "true performance" of the ship. The talk centered on its capability. For as much hype and excitement as there was surrounding the boat, the captain, and the performance – there was a voice of negativity that permeated the crowd. The voice originated from one old lady but spread like wildfire throughout the passengers. She introduced doubt about anything good in the ship and its captain. Though she had been a passenger on the boat and had a great voyage, she wanted to be a voice of negativity.

January 19, 2014

While this vision was rather short, my soul was in a familiar place in the heavens – though I have not described it in detail before. I was talking to an angel who instructed me to go to a baseball card shop in town. This shop would normally be closed, but she said it would stay open late tonight. I walked to the shop, and approached the door. When I got there I could see the hours posted indicated it was closed. As I stood outside, a man opened the door and invited me in. He told me that they would be open later tonight and that it was good to see me again.

The Written (cont'd)

I walked around the store trying to discern what my purpose was. I walked over to a machine that looked like a washing machine. Posted on the outside of the machine was a sign that read "X-Ray/UV Light." It was a warning of sorts, but one that served more as an informational purpose than as a warning. I did not sense anything could happen if I was exposed to the inside of the machine. There was someone already in the machine, and I saw a pale purple light seep out of the seams in the metal.

I kept walking around the store. I eventually picked up a box that was about the size of a cigar box. I looked at the top of the box and tried to read what was written on it. I knew whatever the words said were particular to me and my journey. In the left hand corner, written in a 1970s swirly typeface in light purple and silver glitter were the words, "From Now Until August." I focused on the words and mulled them over in my mind. The words were extremely clear and easy for me to read – which was not typical.

I assumed I must be getting better at understanding communication, words, and archetypes in the heavens. While I focused on the box, I never opened it. I have come to realize that my mind is not curious about the unseen, but only what can be observed directly. Perhaps the box held within it an answer to the words I read. But, in the moment, all I did was concentrate on the words. Eventually, my concentration caused me to lose harmony with everything, and I fell back to Earth.

Rebirth II

January 20, 2014

I am getting tired of having to endure the negative in-between locales that have seemed to be my locations of travel in the heavens recently. So, I have decided it is also best not to acknowledge the negative energy with long, detailed journal entries about the experience. Instead, I will keep the context of the experience brief – highlighting only the points necessary to document the experience.

Last night, I spent a long duration in the heavens. Again, it was in an unsafe area where both good and negative energies have dominion. The setting was a great apartment/condo complex spanning many buildings and many stories. Outside of the buildings, there was a large train track that seemed to be used for entertainment versus necessity. Outside of the setting, suffice it to say, I was chased by negative spirits. I fought them off until I found safety in a unit with angels I recognized. The negative energies tried to introduce doubt into my mind about Lindsey. They emphasized that since she was not in my presence at that moment, that it was not going to work out for us – that I should chalk it up to Love-lost.

When I found the angels, they allowed me to follow, but basically ignored my ramblings of thought. I was trying to rationalize if indeed it was Love-lost, but they just ignored me – suggesting my lack of strength needed to be revisited. While we were there, we walked to a large, formal hall with a great staircase. While there, I saw many cats and small dogs…dogs

The Written (cont'd)

that had been specifically bred to keep them tiny and playful. One dog was small enough to sit on my foot and not fall off when I walked. It stayed there the entire time I walked around even as I began to walk up a flight of stairs.

The angels continued to talk about the name "Del Ray" though I was unsure of the significance. It seemed that we were at a vacation spot in a place called Del Ray, but every cat and dog had the name Del Ray attached to the end of their names. At one point, I saw a cat tumble/slide down the steps and stop before me. I picked it up as the angels asked if it was okay. It was somewhat funny to everyone – myself included – but as we laughed, we made sure the cat was okay. It also had the name Del Ray at the end of its name, though I cannot remember the first name. As I continued to walk up the steps, I noticed the dog sitting on my foot appeared to get heavier – so much that I struggled to walk. Eventually, my struggle led to my mind racing, which caused me to fall out of harmony and return to my body.

January 21, 2014

Last night I experienced three visions, though one of them I was unable to bring back with me. The contents of that particular experience involved walking through the heavens with God talking to me about everything up to this point in my life, and what is planned for me. That is all I can elaborate on that particular experience, though. The second experience in-

Rebirth II

volved me in a vehicle with a motherly angelic figure. She reminded me of my earthly mother, and if I wagered a guess, I would say it was likely her spirit. While we were driving down the road, we were having a conversation about my journey. She seemed adamant that I move from where I lived. It was very important to her that I do not stay in the place I currently reside. I took her comments to mean the Nashville area, and nothing more specific. However, she never specified the meaning. I tried to change the subject a couple of times because it did not seem that it was quite time for me to leave Nashville during my journey, and I did not want to have conflict in conversation. I asked her what she thought about me using a particular guitarist to record the guitar parts on a handful of songs for me and to fix one that I had recorded earlier in my life. She told me it was a terrible idea. In that moment, I could tell she did not like my music. I could tell she did not want me to have any attachment to Nashville. I told her it did not matter what she felt because I knew there was a purpose for me staying a bit longer. She continued to get upset with me. I eventually told her this is where we will need to part ways for a while. I got out of the vehicle and walked up the exit ramp on the interstate. I wandered to a large building and walked inside. The inside was much like a hotel where the hallways and apartments all opened into a center atrium. I walked up several flights of stairs, and as I was heading down a hallway I heard a shout from below asking me if I was staying. I shouted back that I was and that we should catch up soon. He told me,

The Written (cont'd)

"That's great to hear. Georgia will be happy with it." The vision faded and I returned to my earthly body.

    The next vision was brief. I was standing in my condo with the wall of glass windows on my left. In front of me was a group of kids lying in a grid. There were three rows of four kids each. Their heads were in the west, there bodies pointing east. The moon was full and shining down through the windows. They each were holding up something that resembled a mirror or a mobile phone. The moon was in the west and was being captured by whatever it was they were holding. Perhaps they were viewing the moon's reflection in a mirror. One child joked that it was "the first time [they had] ever seen someone take "selfies" of the sun." Another child said, "It is the only way a person can reach heaven. It is how it was done by the ancients." I kind of laughed as I walked over to them. I told them, "You are indeed right – that the moon would allow their body and soul to separate and travel the heavens." They all looked at me as if I was their teacher. The moment lingered a little longer before I lost harmony with the moment and returned to my body.

January 22, 2014

    I remember very little (at best) from last night. I can remember two distinct portions of visions: the first of which involved me talking about a certain song called, "The Rose." I talked with an angel about how it was funny that I listened to

Rebirth II

it so much as a child because my mother Loved it, and now I find myself full-circle enjoying a new piano version of it that recently came out. I know we talked for a while on the subject of how childhood moments will circle back in the days of spiritual growth, but the conversation is hazy for me to recall. The second vision only left me with one resounding memory. At the very end of a conversation with an angel, I was told that the timeline had shifted for me and "to plan for July, not August." I wish I could recall the context, but I cannot. I have recently shifted my sleep routine, and I think that the shift has caused my body to fall out of sync with the greatest energy alignments of the sun and the moon. I am going to try to get myself back into my original routine – hopefully that will help with the clarity.

January 23, 2014

The visions of the night came in great frequency again. However, I am still struggling with finding synchrony with my altered sleep schedule. My spirit and body seem to be fighting each other as to who gets priority when the time is right to journey to the heavens. Last night was no different. There was one point I awoke in my body with a great burst of energy. This is the second night this has happened – which means I just experienced something marvelous, though my mind did not allow me to bring it back with me. To be suddenly startled awake with that particular feeling has only happened during

The Written (cont'd)

some of the most divine moments I have ever experienced with angels and with God. I can only imagine that they are helping coax me back into synchrony while I realign my sleep schedule around this time. The remainder of the night was filled with small, sporadic visions – and one great one. One of the smaller visions involved an angel telling me a specific sentence regarding Lindsey. It began with "Lindsey Baker Knight, the one who…" I was confident that I would remember the sentence in its entirety when I returned to my body – and I did for quite some time. I lay awake thinking about everything in the sentence for nearly an hour before trying to return to the heavens. But, upon returning, I forgot the last half of the sentence. The important part is that it emphasized her last name as Knight. This is a call out to a chapter in my book called, "Dance of Knight" as well as a shout out to the encounter with the Dove and Hawk that God placed in my life a few weeks ago (written about in the chapter "The Dove & The Hawk"). Both chapters can be found in the book I am writing called "Gravity Calling." Essentially, the rest of the sentence I cannot remember in full, indicated her last name was Knight, symbolizing everything I have come to know about her placement in my life by the hand of God. For, my spiritual body has yet to have been given a name. So, if God wanted to indicate our unity on Earth through symbolism, it would be done with something letting me know that she and I end up together. In this case, the chapter in my book refers to me as a "knight" – so Lindsey having Knight as her last name indicates our future spiritual union.

Rebirth II

The second experience was filled with extreme sensitivity to the surroundings. Sometimes spiritual experiences are dull with respect to the Earthy senses, and sometimes they are overpoweringly strong. In this case, every sensation was extremely heightened. I sat across from an angel in a classroom. No one else was in the room – it was just her and me. This was the same angel that has maternal characteristics. Something about her teeth reminded me of my mother, so that is possibly why I am identifying her as such. After the experience today, I now know she is my instructor – my guide for this part of the journey. She is teaching me the skills I will need to better serve as a bridge between the two peoples of the heavens and the Earth. While sitting across from her, she told me to tell her something serious. She was staring deeply into my eyes, and I into hers. Her eyes were a broken-crystal blue. Her question was an invitation for me to help her bring her mind down to a lower frequency. All I could think of was the worst possible thing. For some reason, as I looked into her eyes I became aware that she had lost a child somewhere along the way. I concentrated on it, debating whether saying anything about that was appropriate or the expected answer. As she noticed I was now aware of this moment, her eyes began to quiver. I knew the thought was heavy on her heart and now recognized they were words I should not say. But, it was too late. By looking into each other's eyes we had somehow connected our minds. She knew precisely what I was thinking about telling her. She said, "I know what you want to say." I responded quickly, "No. I can't. I'm still thinking about it." I could tell

The Written (cont'd)

words were no longer required for the lesson. By thought alone, her vibratory level was brought down to the level she needed for the lesson. She stood up, breaking eye contact. She walked by my right shoulder in a manner to grab my attention, making slight contact in her rush. As she walked, her body faded away. I turned to look for her. I could tell the path she walked by a hazy outline left in her wake. I quickly found where she had stopped. She was standing in front of a window having walked in an arc from her chair of about 250 degrees. Her spirit was translucent, but I could see its affect by way of light refraction of the surroundings. As soon as I saw her I became extremely excited. I shouted out, "You did it!" It was one of those moments my body was so overcome with excitement, my spiritual body and my physical body reacted together. As I shouted out the words, my mind raced with excitement causing me to lose harmony and drawing my spirit back to my earthly body. I lay in bed trying to shout out the words. Eventually my vocal chords allowed the words to erupt in clarity causing me to immediately awaken. Realizing what had just happened, I lay there thinking about the moment. It was clear the lesson was on bringing the vibratory level down so that my guide could remain hidden from her surroundings. She was still noticeable, but only by those with a clever eye who knew what to look for in the refraction. I am sure there will be much more to be gleaned from this as to how it applies to my earthly walk, the symbolism, the potential physical manifestation of what I saw, but for now, it was quite the experience.

Rebirth II

January 24, 2014

I experienced a conversation with a peculiar man in my heavenly experience who claimed he was from the future. In the beginning, I thought it was my granddad – but after reflecting on the entire scenario, I am not completely sure that it was. The man was very small, about half of the height of everyone else – myself included. When he approached me, he was very excited to see me, but overcome with an exuberance of thoughts that he struggled to get out as quickly as they were firing in his mind. He came up and grabbed my hand to get my attention and then began telling me almost in a panic about an impending event that I needed to hear – needed to understand. I just looked at him quizzically. He began to explain how he could "travel further than most people" and then further elaborated that he meant "travel into the future further than most people." He explained to me that there would be a "family event from a natural disaster" that would occur "a week or so from now." I asked him, "Aren't there systems in place to let us know of such a natural disaster?" He was oddly excited in his response and said, "Of course there are. This warning system is one of six great programs that had been worked on," but he also said that the public was unaware of any of the programs existences. As we talked about the situation, he never elaborated in specifics as to what the disaster would be. He did mention that some of the other programs were "Cement bursting explosions, and concrete forming ex-

The Written (cont'd)

plosions." My impression was that these were somewhat equivalent to bunker buster bombs and some type of explosion that immediately turned everything into a concrete or solid matter...sort of like the cold fusion device used in the second Star Trek movie to prevent the volcano from blowing up. Though I did not ask many questions that received direct answers to his scattered thoughts, he continued to re-emphasize the natural disaster would be the worst recent mankind has ever known and that it is already known about in inner circles, just to be revealed to the public in this "week or so" timeframe. He did not tell me what form though. As the words continued to soak in, it sent my spirit spinning back to my earthly body as I lost harmony with the moment.

 A second experience in the heavens occurred on a restaurant's outside veranda. There were two angels there with me. One seemed to be there specifically for me. The other seemed to be there for someone else whom I never saw. The angel that was there for me had blonde hair. She was extremely tall and had a very short haircut. It is the kind of haircut that is longer in the front around the face, but chopped off in an angle on the back, so that the base of the hairline on the neck is nearly shaved, and halfway up the head it is back to normal thickness. She was excited about her haircut, though I did not like it very much. I have always preferred long hair, so I just observed, not commenting at all. She showed her hair off to her friend. They had been talking about it when I arrived. They had apparently been waiting on me. As I arrived, they were very excited about introducing me to someone. The blonde angel

Rebirth II

told the other to get us "two tables with romantic seating." For some reason it appeared we were on some sort of date. Soon another angel arrived. She had brown hair. They introduced her to me as Audra. As I said, "I'm Jonathan," they commented to themselves, giggling. I knew I was giving my earthly name, but since I have yet to be told an angelic name, that is all I have to work with. As we were talking, I began to get cold (which typically happens as my earthly body begins to overheat). I commented about forgetting my coat. They laughed. I could tell I was entertaining them. As we began to have dinner, I tried to piece together everything happening in the moment. Who was this Audra person? Who were these angels? I seemed to interact with these angels a lot recently, but I wanted to understand how it applied to my earthly life as well. I was not satisfied with the duality of the two spaces anymore it seemed. As we waited on dinner, I turned the conversation to church, and I asked about what church I would be going to. They laughed and said, "I don't know. I assume Franklin." I was hoping they would relate it to something in my earthly walk, but they did not. I am not sure what the Franklin church is – but that is what I was told, so I pondered the thought. I debated in my mind what the setting in the heavens was and if "Franklin" possibly referred to the city of Franklin near Nashville. The thought ended up causing me to lose harmony and I returned to my body.

The Written (cont'd)

January 26, 2014

As I was in the heavens, I found myself before an angel and a child. They were both female. I noticed that the child had dyed her hair blond, and so had the angel. The child was extremely proud of her hair. I asked her why she had dyed her hair. The child told me, "I wanted to be beautiful, so I wanted blonde hair." I told her that she could be just as beautiful with brown hair if she wanted to be. Then I looked at her mother – the angelic figure before me. I said, "I see you have dyed your hair too again." It was evident the child saw her mother as beautiful and wanted to do everything the mother did. The angel just smiled at me and said that she had. She told me that she wanted to feel happy again. She then showed me how short it actually was from behind. It was deceivingly short. From the front, it looked long. But from the back, it had that same angled cut I observed in my previous vision. I tried to decide if it was the same angel, but could not determine if it was. In both cases, the blonde hair was clearly dyed and the underneath color was a natural dark brown. The deeper I thought, the more I lost harmony and fell out of the heavens.

After journaling the previous experience, I returned to the heavens. I found myself having lunch in a food court in a mall. This mall has been recurring throughout my visions, but again, this may be one of those settings that I have not written about before. It always plays out very similarly with me running into a brunette artist after I wander through the food

Rebirth II

court. But this time was a little different. As I observed the room, I noticed that all of the people were very business-oriented. I was sharing a table with a large group of other business executives. As we ate, some were dismissed from the table. Some stayed. I could not find rationale to who was staying or leaving, so I just watched. I eventually decided that I would leave since I was finished eating. As I walked away, I heard my name shouted. It was the brunette artist friend I see regularly in this setting. She was very happy to see me. I joked about us always running into each other in the mall. She asked why I was always there, but I danced around the answer because – honestly, I quite simply did not know. I was not sure how to say, "This is just where I travel to sometimes in the heavens." I asked if she was buying art supplies. It made her smile. She said, "Of course," and then proceeded to show me frames and supplies in a large bag she was holding. She kept emphasizing that it was really good to see me. We eventually parted ways, and I decided to wander around the mall. I found an entrance to a theatre, and as I headed in, I saw a group of angels I knew. These were the angels that continued to recur in the last several weeks of visions (if not months). As we walked into the seating area before the movie started, a girl suddenly appeared behind me. It was the blonde haired angel. I felt extremely glad to see her. I always feel a close bond when she is around. The angels ahead of me tried to find a group of seats for all of us, but there was not a section large enough. I thought that would be okay because it would give me time to sit down with the blonde angel alone. She was wearing a black

The Written (cont'd)

dress and small blue hat. We eventually found two seats in the corner and were chatting. She told me that she had just lost her father. She was extremely upset, and I could tell the dress that she was wearing must have been for the funeral. As much as I tried to help her or lend my heart and soul, it did not seem to work. She did not want to hear anything. She was too shaken. Nothing I could do was working. She eventually became overwhelmed by her emotions and wanted to leave. I followed her out trying to comfort her, but she headed on anyway. It was then I returned to my body from the heavens.

After journaling the previous experience, I returned to the heavens for a third time. Every one of these experiences lasted much longer than the notes entail, but I cannot always manage to hold onto the entire amount of information in the moments following returning to my body. This next experience is again one of those situations. It must have lasted hours of earthly time, but I could only bring back the highlights. It began in a very nice restaurant – a five-star kind of place. I was eating with an extremely large group of angels at one large banquet table. There were maybe twenty or more angels together. It was a group I do not normally socialize with in the heavens, but find myself interacting with them from time to time. They are all extremely beautiful and often intimidating to me. There is one brunette girl that stands out beyond everyone else in the group. She sometimes is the brunette angel that works with me personally. I think it must be Anael or Arielle, though I have not asked her since that one day a year or so ago when I was told I had upset them. While I was there, I

Rebirth II

had the memory of a conversation prior to arriving at the restaurant. It was with the spirit of Jason – an old friend on Earth. He asked me who I go out with these days. He was puzzled that he never saw me anymore. I knew this was his spirit talking to me about his recent odd questions to me on Earth. We were once the closest of friends but fell apart as I experienced my genesis and subsequent journey into the light. I told his spirit that I do a lot by myself these days, but every now and then one of the male angels in that group invites me out with them. Jason was envious of the group. I could tell that he wanted in the group, though I could not tell if it was a desire to be in that particular circle of souls, or if it was because we once spent a lot of time together and now that group was my outlet for friends. I did not tell him in that moment, but I wanted to let him know that I always found that group lacking something my soul longed for – except for the brunette, who was always mesmerizing to me. But, I knew the group enjoyed my company when I was around, so I always went when invited. While we were eating, a group went upstairs to take some celebratory "shots" or whatever the equivalent would be in the heavens. I did not want to partake – and it is also partly why I find a divide with that particular group. I excused myself and went to the bathroom. It was small and had green walls and dark walnut wood trim. The single toilet inside had a dark walnut door as well. I waited for the person before me to come out, which took an abnormally long amount of time. He eventually exited and I entered. As soon as I went in, I noticed another door. I entered. I found myself in a secret room, full of

The Written (cont'd)

the holiest of angels. The room was large, with white alabaster walls and tall ceilings. It seemed almost like a "control room" compared to the restaurant setting from before. Perhaps the experiences are getting tough to describe now because I have to define the heavens as separate from the Earth, and the angelic forms of people versus their human counterparts. But if I could describe this particular group of angels versus the other angels I was with earlier, I would have to say this is a higher level of "holy." The group I was with was a group of angels that seemed to be on a tier that much more parallels with earthly bodies, though some show glimmers of being holier than others. I wish there were clearer definitions, but that is the best I can do at this point. So, anyway, as I stood in this room full of angels, they welcomed me in and enjoyed my company. They were glad I had found them, and we chatted for a while. I came to realize this is why the guy in the bathroom before me took such a long time. He had also found the entrance and enjoyed their company. Eventually I had to return. When I found my way out of the room and left the bathroom, I realized I was walking barefooted. I decided I must have left my shoes behind in the bathroom, but I did not recall taking them off. I went back in and saw two pairs of shoes on the floor in front of the bathroom stall door. I tried them on and realized neither pair was mine. I reached under the door to see if my shoes had slid into the stall. Right at that point someone behind the door slid my shoes out. I never saw the person or angel, but I thanked them. I put my shoes on and walked out. The group that had gone upstairs to get

Rebirth II

drinks was returning. They asked where I went. I mentioned that I went in the bathroom, but did not tell them what I had experienced. I decided it was time for me to depart, so I said my good-byes and left the restaurant just as my soul returned to my body.

January 27, 2014

While the events of this vision were extremely long and detailed, I feel like the amount of realism overwhelmed me. As soon as I returned to my body, I began to journal about the experience, but struggled to recall any of the details. While I cannot recall the events with clarity leading up to what I am about to describe, this was another vision that lasted for hours, if not days. But what I am able to recall is standing in a great trial room, or government room. There was a huge, towering double level desk before me made of a shimmering metallic white. It was a substance I have not seen before on Earth and find it difficult to describe. It was sort of like a high gloss paint, but metallic…and white. The desk was concave and must have been twenty feet tall or larger. If it was 20 feet tall, it must have been 40 feet wide. There were large angels sitting on each of the levels. A lower level of about half the height was in front. The desk sat approximately ten to twelve great angels. It was something that I could only describe as a formal assembly of upper level members of some official establishment. I was standing before them. It was not as if I was on trial, but

The Written (cont'd)

there was a definite reason I was before them. I felt that they were determining if I was ready and capable for the next part of my journey. But, to put the complexity of thought and feeling I had in that moment into that paltry of a summation makes me really wish I had words to describe the feeling. But as I stood before them, I began to observe the desk in more detail. There was a sign that was not legible in the very center – directly beneath the angel in charge. There were two other markings on the desk that I could see. One stood out immediately. It was the number 1556. It was clearly legible. The other one was much more blurry, but the numbers resembled 1776, though the last number may not have been a 6. It was the hardest to read of the four numbers. As I concentrated on the 1776 word, my attention was called back to the superior angel. He saw I was reading everything on the desk, though I was still standing where I originally was in the center before them. He acted as if I should not be able to read it; therefore, I should not be trying. There was another angel on the bottom left that smiled when he recognized that I had read it with accuracy, or at least three of the four numbers. If it is 1776, this is the second time it has occurred in recent visions. The other time it occurred, I also wrote about it. But as my attention was called back, I lost harmony and my soul returned to my body.

    After journaling and returning to the heavens, I found myself wandering the streets of a city at night. It was familiar to me. I saw a small bar/music venue that I recognized. I went in. It was no larger than 15 x 30 with extremely tall ceilings. I sat down and listened to a girl play an instrument that resem-

Rebirth II

bled a guitar and sing. It was not anyone special, but I was very moved by the music. As she finished, a small group of five or six people shuffled in the door with excitement about what was about to occur. The owner looked outside to see if anyone else was coming and saw that the whole group had entered. He locked the door and turned around and faced me with the same excitement on his face that the others in the group exuded. The owner made an announcement that someone very special was in the room. It was a red-haired angel who was standing directly by my right shoulder. With the people that had entered, the space became quite cramped, so there was not any room to move. I was excited to be standing beside the angel. She smiled at me when I looked at her. She seemed like some sort of celebrity to everyone. She seemed to be accompanied by another angel, who was one of her friends. He was also of similar fame and a musician. Apparently this was a special surprise night where they wanted to have an intimate performance without anyone else knowing and causing a ruckus. The male angel began playing very beautiful music. I could hear it, but I was confused because I did not see him on stage. It became my understanding that the red-haired angel was going to sing duets with him. It was a day of celebration for her. The owner asked me what I thought about it all. I felt like the one person in the room that should not be there. Everyone else knew each other, and I was just alone when they all came rushing in the door. I did not want to tell him that, so of course I told him I was glad to be there and that I was surprised by what unfolded. He was proud. He told me I should

The Written (cont'd)

find the guy singing. I wandered around the small confines of the room, but was never able to find where the song came from. I kept thinking it came from a ledge/small patio that was raised above the floor, but I could not see over the edge from below. I also had no idea how to reach it. I decided to walk outside and observe the building. When I did, the outside immediately transformed into a long corridor with three giant angels standing before a doorway at the end of the hall. They were guardians to something divine. They seemed austere and slightly irritated when I approached. I wanted to tell them what I had just experienced but struggled to put my thoughts into words. The main guardian in the middle kept asking me what I wanted to say. I eventually managed to say, "Nothing. It isn't important now. I'll ask you later." Those were the only words I could say with confidence. All other words were failing me. They allowed me to enter though I did not quite know where I was going. I scurried past them and lost harmony, returning to my body.

January 28, 2014

Even in the warm, blissful weather of Haiti, I found I still could not escape the cold permanently. In my first trip to the heavens this morning, I found myself standing in the middle of a great snowstorm. I knew that the location was "back home" and that it was not "Nashville." I realized that while I was experiencing perfect weather in Haiti, it seemed as if my family

Rebirth II

in Georgia was being plagued with snowfall. Even in Nashville, we had not experienced much, if any, snow this year, so I thought the message of snowfall in Georgia was somewhat off-kilter if it was expressing an earthly truth. I chalked it up to just a demonstration of extremes in the weather. I enjoyed the snow in the experience. I ice skated around the heavens and eventually skated over toward a hockey player. The rest is very hazy at best. I do not recall much else before I returned back to my body.

Upon returning to Nashville, I learned that on the day of this experience in the heavens, the Atlanta area was hit with an unforeseen snow and ice storm that caused businesses to shut down for three days. The storm did not hit Nashville, but rather affected my family living in the Atlanta area. When I saw the news story, I was not surprised – but it was one of the rare times I have known I was allowed the opportunity to experience (at least archetypally) something occurring in another part of the world without any knowledge of the matter at hand.

After journaling the experience, I returned to the heavens. I spoke with the spirit of Jon – my supervisor at work. He was unhappy having to rush completion of the presentation. I told him I knew he was unhappy, but I have always executed well, and this time would be no different. The experience was short lived and I returned to journal the conversation.

Upon returning to work the following week, Jon called me into his office to push forward a presentation I had due in a couple of weeks. He was frustrated at a lot of the reasoning

The Written (cont'd)

behind it, though the presentation was not shifted by his choice. I could sense his frustration. It turned out that during my absence, the CIO was fired and a new CIO had stepped in. This new CIO was pushing the executive leaders to expedite upcoming presentations/etc. so that he could get caught up on the state of affairs. Again, this reality on Earth was mirrored in the heavens several days prior.

I returned to the heavens again after journaling the previous experience. I found myself standing in a city-like location with a brunette girl. She was pretty, but something seemed off about the situation. Her name was Audra (side note – I do not know anyone named Audra on Earth). Audra "lived an hour away from me" and wanted to date me. She was very forthright with her intentions, though she emphasized that we should start slowly as friends. This was an unusual experience in the heavens, but I figured there was no harm in going on a date with her, so I obliged. Something just seemed off the whole time. I could not put my finger on it exactly, but it was as if the whole incident was forced. Anyway, for our date, we met at a location that I had never seen before in the heavens. Her parents were sitting at a table enjoying a coffee (or something similar). We spoke our introductions and eventually parted ways. For some reason, she wanted her daughter to spend time with her family, so I let that happen as well. Audra was very methodical in everything – and perhaps that is why it seemed "off." She wanted to make sure she scheduled the time with my daughter and her family. There was a strict schedule that had to be followed. The experience ended with me having

Rebirth II

allowed my daughter to spend time with her parents, and Audra and I having a mismatched date. It was apparent, but she really wanted to see if it would work. After it ended, I returned to my body.

In my final experience in the heavens this morning, I was shown a vision of a great tidal wave coming toward me and everyone in the city. I found a female angel that I was supposed to save. We raced up to the top of a mountain. Along the way, we had to run through a city that reminded me of an old Biblical city. The walls were stone. The streets were cobblestone. The city was built upon the mountain, so it was important to take the shortest route to the top of the mountain. We passed through doors that were specific for "Jewish people." These doors were shortcuts to the destination where others were not allowed to pass. I am not Jewish, so understand that the imagery and experience were illustrating something important to bring back to Earth. Eventually, we made it to the top of the mountain. I was standing amongst a small group of people. They seemed unhappy I was there. I explained I was there because "I had God inside of me." At this point, the experience became very spiritual. Eventually, Jesus showed up as the leader of the group. I had never seen Jesus in a vision – at least not where I could identify him as Jesus. There had been times I had experienced angels that left me wondering if one was Jesus. But this time, it was clear who He was. As Jesus addressed the group, He spoke very highly of me and built my rapport with the group of people disheartened to see me. It was as if they had to hear the words from

The Written (cont'd)

Him to acknowledge that I did have "God inside of me." Jesus asked me to lead a prayer with the group. I led the group and watched as many were confused at what it was I had found within me. I understood the group to be disciples of Jesus. The word "disciple" was used repeatedly. After I led the prayer, Jesus continued to address the group. He asked me to speak to them, but I was shy to speak out loud in front of Jesus. There was an inordinate amount of pressure I felt – a gravity to the weight my words carried and the delicacy of which I was to carefully use them. Eventually Jesus had to leave, but he made sure the group understood that I was the leader. After he left, I led the group, speaking boldly to them. It helped me build my confidence as an orator, and this particular experience had so many layers of depth that my mind reeled in the experience. Nightfall would eventually come and I returned to my body to journal the experience.

January 29, 2014

This morning in the heavens I witnessed an elderly couple who had lost their physical form. They were so much in Love and though they were formless, I witnessed them making Love outside over and over again. They were lost in a blissful romance. The only way I could categorize their Lovemaking was that it was "on a whim" with no concerns around them. I watched as the elderly woman dropped her clothes in front of the man who was sitting on a stool at an outside bar. He was

Rebirth II

reading a newspaper. She immediately made it clear she wanted him. She was in her 80s though it is difficult to explain how she had form, but had lost her physical form. Her body had gained weight in the midsection and everything sagged unfavorably. My best understanding was I was seeing how her physical form was meaningless in the heavens because they were uniting in a perfect union of mind, body, and spirit. What I witnessed is what I believe every person has longed to experience in youthful play, though I witnessed it in age. Their souls demonstrated the passions of youth. Their souls knew no age. And that was the importance I was to observe. I watched as Love filled the surroundings while they experienced the Love between each other.

I returned to the heavens and found myself in a scenario that reminded me of something out of the show Dexter. It was dark and brooding and foretold of a disturbing reality. I was just an observer, but I was supposed to understand that this situation had actually occurred in real life – as if I was witnessing a murderer's life from another time and place. The overriding theme of the experience was that the villain appeared to be the hero. I was never scared although I felt constantly sick to my stomach witnessing everything I saw.

When I arrived back in the heavens, I watched as a boy in a boathouse received a phone call. I could not hear the conversation or the voice on the other side, but in response he repeatedly pressed numbers on the keypad. Eventually it became evident that the voice on the other side was tired of waiting for his desires to be done correctly, so it manifested in

The Written (cont'd)

form at the boathouse. The child became scared and ran away. I rode in the car with the man who appeared to chase the boy. I flashed forward in time and saw the child as a young 20 year old desiring to have his face recognized in a police station. I then saw a young version of the child visiting the police station on a field trip for school. He saw a bust of someone in bronze and embraced the idea that he would one day be well known that way. As the group of students left, I watched as a person a few car lengths ahead became the boy's victim of choice. He followed after his target. Eventually the pickup truck realized it was being followed and panicked. The pickup truck started driving fast and carelessly through crowds of people in an effort to lose his tail. A person was hit in the process. And, while they would have survived, they landed in front of the child driver who took his urge to kill and ran over the guy's skull crushing it into a million pieces. The two pickup trucks halted. The evil driver had blood splattered across his doorway and on his arm that was hanging outside of the window. There was a brief exchange of words and an awkward stare down. An officer came up to the evil child after he had cleaned up most of the mess. The child acted like a helpless victim. I was disgusted the officer fell for it.

The second vision involved a male angel that reminded me of Tim McGraw. It was much more pleasant and made me feel Love – a spring break kind of Love. I was some sort of a tag-along and not just an observer. I watched as his interactions with people made their hearts resonate in song. I saw his wife hopelessly in Love with him. Eventually we found our-

Rebirth II

selves in the back row of a concert lying on benches. He was on the back row slightly above me. The male angel was lying on his stomach. His wife was sitting near his legs on the same row. I was laying on my stomach as well, one bench lower. Suddenly a song came on and I felt my spirit move. It was a song about a girl in blue jeans – one I had never heard. The lyrics that kept repeating were along the lines of "sundown nearing its end (you better take care) and it's a fine time to see (ain't she a sight to see) that blue jean baby has got the best of me. (That blue jean baby is the best kind of beautiful to me)." The lyrics in parentheses were alternate versions of the chorus. It repeated several times. My body moved with the song. I became aware that the seats we were lying across were in the spotlight of someone's eye. The male angel took the lead and made sure his movements were exaggerated as someone would typically see in a music video of someone falling in Love. My body moved in the same way. I writhed and moved according to how my soul felt led. My mind filled with Lindsey and a picture I recently saw of her in blue jeans. Every time I saw the image, I felt a pinch in the lower right portion of my back....on the fringe of the crest of my buttocks. It felt very sexual, very romantic. As I envisioned the picture of Lindsey, the twinge felt like a gentle nibble with teeth. I became aware that another female angel that had been sitting with us was making sure I received the message that was trying to be conveyed. I am not sure if she was really biting me or just giving me a twinge so that I would remember the moment, but it was effective. The twinge caused me to recognize an erogenous zone on my body

The Written (cont'd)

that I was previously unaware existed. It also showed me a method to give rise to the particular feeling flooding my body at that moment. But most importantly, the words were important for me to remember regarding Lindsey. It was not just in the lyrics I could recall, but in the overarching theme of the song and how the words gave rise to feelings of Love, and Love gave rise to the tremendous energy within. The third angel that joined us was an angel with sandy blonde hair that reappears every so often. It is important to know that the word "sundown" was a divine reference to words I penned earlier today about my spiritual journey. Also, the end lyrics hinted at lyrics from a song I wrote a long time ago called "Best Kind of Beautiful."

I returned once again to the heavens where the same song was played over and over again in its entirety until I lost harmony and returned to my body.

January 30, 2014

I arrived in a city in the heavens. I was being escorted around by a male angel. He took me to "someone great's funeral." It was important for me to witness the funeral. For some reason, I thought it was a girl's funeral. The coffin was to be laid to rest just near the building we were standing in. The cemetery was located just behind the building to the right. The building we were in was an old stone chapel with long oak pews. There were only a few people there to witness the funer-

Rebirth II

al. After the service, I watched as a small white coffin was carried behind a caravan by just one person. It seemed almost like a celebration instead of a funeral. Shortly after the small white coffin passed by, a large coffin encased in black graphite passed by, carried in the back of a limo. The person in this coffin was not celebrated as the other person was. I thought it was odd because I thought the body had already passed by us. Though the two coffins were definitely part of the same funeral progression, the duality of the moment confused me. I could tell the white coffin contained a child and was celebrated, while the black coffin contained an adult and was barely acknowledged. As I pondered the events of the funeral, the people around me spoke of everyone going to lunch. Even though these individuals that were all in the church sat separately from each other – each experiencing the funeral in his own way, it was now apparent that everyone knew each other and were friends. This was another oddity to the funeral progression. Eventually my earthly alarm went off and drew my soul back to my body from the heavens.

February 1, 2014

Lindsey has obviously been a focal point in my life. Whether the entire episode is a lesson God is using for me to learn about Love and to hear His voice, to test my ability to follow His directions, I cannot be sure. But the important thing is that this is the reality around me at the present mo-

The Written (cont'd)

ment – a reality wherein I have learned to hear God's voice more intimately while finding a way to speak to Him in a way I was unable prior. The thoughts racing through my mind most recently have been an effort to help me understand whether it was up to my spiritual actions to invoke Lindsey into my life or wait on God. The experience this morning began to elaborate on my dilemma. My travels to the heavens began with me standing next to a beautiful blonde angel. At first she presented herself to me as Lindsey, but that was only to grab my attention. We walked through several different coffee shops as I sought to understand His signs around me. We walked past a table where an angel was writing on a piece of paper. I looked down to see what the angel was writing about. The writing was entitled "Silence." It was chapter 25 (which I recognized in that moment how 2 + 5 summed to 7 – a divine sign). I understood that it was my role to maintain silence and just enjoy the ride. We eventually parted ways where I found myself outside of a condo, walking across a beautiful bay bridge on my way to a restaurant. I passed a gorgeous glass office building unlike any I have ever seen. I found a restaurant that I wanted to try. Just outside of the establishment, I felt something in my shoe and sat down to remove the object. As I searched for the object, I observed a lady talking about how she does not make any money and was not being served food. She was waiting for the owner, who finally came out to speak with her. They had an argument about who serves whom. I went inside. Upstairs was the location of the restaurant I wanted to try. The downstairs area was a bar and BBQ

Rebirth II

place. I did not initially recognize the building as holding two restaurants until I wandered around in search of a place to sit. I walked upstairs, and back down. When I reached the bottom I saw the seats and everyone eating and realized it was two places. I walked back to the stairs to find a seat. When I reached the stairs, I realized I could no longer climb the stairs. I was too tired. I saw what appeared to be my mother and her best friend sit down at a table near me, but they did not recognize me. Undeterred, I walked over and said hello. We talked for a few and then my mom decided to go for a run. I followed behind. As we ran, I noticed that roads were periodically shut down for runners. Eventually I stopped to sit down and rest. I saw a floating bundle of balloons of Santa and his reindeer, which made me curious. I decided to head over in the direction of the balloons. On a level above the road I was on, a lady was storing balloons in a brick storage building. There was a couple outside asking about her rate. She explained she had the run down storage shed listed as a hotel so she could put it on her insurance instead of being charged more for a storage unit. The couple thought it was clever, but she joked that it might cause legal trouble down the way. She noticed me standing there and invited me inside. As I wandered through the building I eventually came to a stop at the end of a long hallway. There was a mirror before me but I did not want to look into it. I felt a lady touch my right shoulder. Her hand lingered. I knew she was trying to see into my soul. I tried to see into hers. She placed her other hand on my left shoulder. We stood there like that for a few moments. Eventually I

The Written (cont'd)

sensed a great force passing through us. There was a loud burst of sound like something from a sci-fi movie along with a purple burst of light, and I suddenly found myself in my body. Not content with the ending, I travelled back. This time, I was much more exhausted and tired than when I had left. I arrived in a bedroom. Each time I tried to leave the room I felt a strange sensation at the threshold of the door. I knew that if I crossed the door I would lose harmony. I lay in bed and began to contemplate all of the activity I had experienced. Suddenly, a cat jumped on the bed and began walking all over me. It finally found its way to my face and continued stepping on it. The frustration sent my soul back to my body and I awoke. I recognized the last two "bursts" were trying to get me back to Earth, though I am not sure why it was with so much force.

February 4, 2014

The experience in the heavens began with me ice-skating. This scenario is becoming increasingly more common. In the beginning I could barely skate. But, over the course of the heavenly experiences, I have continued to progress at skating and at playing hockey. I have to think that the concepts of hockey and ice-skating must serve as symbolism to the movement of the spirit and the concept of motion. Once the ability to maintain fluid motion is achieved, then it is important to hone the skills of a player to a sport, for the experience of being a spiritual steward is similar to playing a game against

Rebirth II

others. Anyway, this experience began with me in the midst of a hockey game. I scored a goal in the game, and everyone was excited. They invited me to take more shots on goal because I had proven myself worthy. I no longer felt that I was sitting on the sidelines while they played (as I have in other visions). I have also been put in the games during the closing minutes of the game just to get experience. It is the same type of experience athletes experience when they move from junior varsity into a varsity sport, from high school to college, from college to professional sports. During one portion of the game, I experienced one great play that I am sure holds a metaphorical meaning to my spiritual journey. I was the trailing player on an attack on the opponent's goal. I had to wait for the forwards to skate down and perform a "920°." I do not know why they had to perform that type of move, but it was important to remember the number. Once they performed their move, I was supposed to slice through the middle of the players to receive the pass and shoot. The experience was hyper real. I could feel every sensation with heightened reality. I performed the move and scored. It was important to know that after performing the move and scoring that I "could become rookie of the year" at the age of "only" thirty-three.

    The next experience in the heavens placed me in a situation where I chatted with a man about a new job. It was a man that had a voice similar to a person I spoke with on the phone recently. We chatted about my work history, and I demonstrated past projects. I was offered the job doing iOS programming. Up to that point, I was serving as some sort of a

The Written (cont'd)

fitness instructor in a rehab facility. It was a lot like a gym, but more focused on classes and training. The walls and floors were covered in red-plank cedar.

When I returned from Haiti, I received three messages on my phone – two asking me to be an iOS programmer. One of the calls later progressed to the job I accepted on 3/20 – but there is much more that will be written about it at a later point.

February 5, 2014

While brief, I was sitting behind a car. I noticed that the license plate was one that I had never seen before. I realized that I was in a foreign place (as would be the case since I was in the heavens). While I am sure it was supposed to be a queue for my soul to recognize I was in the heavens so I could have further experiences, my mind caused me to lose harmony and I returned to my body.

February 6, 2014

Though the details are sparse, my travels to the heavens this morning lasted for what seemed like hours upon hours. In the heavens, I was playing a game where I was being hunted. And while I never felt like I could die, the scenario played out like a real-world battle. There were soldiers, militia, and bullets that whizzed by as I sought cover in the woods. I eventually found my way to a quaint cottage in the countryside. But even in the cottage, bullets still continued to fly past me.

February 8, 2014

In this morning's vision, I found myself in a completely destroyed city. It was post-apocalyptic. Two angels accompanied me as we tried to find a way to survive. Every house we went into was somehow in the crosshairs of the next bombing raid from the planes above. The planes were trying to exterminate anyone of the angels that still existed. When the planes first arrived, the angels thought the planes were there to rescue us. But as the planes neared, it was obvious they were there to continue destroying the area. The planes would navigate around the city. At any sign of life, they would drop bombs in an effort to ensure there were no survivors. In the rubble I could see lots of dead bodies that had rotted and melted in the sun.

February 9, 2014

The experience began with me standing in the presence of three angels. We were in a store that was hosting some form of a party. The angels all acknowledged my presence and were very excited to see me. The angels were all extremely beautiful, and it warmed my heart that I was not just in the presence

The Written (cont'd)

of angels, but in the presence of angels genuinely excited to see me.

The final travel to the heavens ended with me in the backyard of a house. The stars were overhead without a cloud in sight. The wind was at a standstill. Everything about the moment seemed perfect. I was in the presence of two other male angels. We were going to participate in a triune type of worship. It required three guys to meditate to feel God's Love. Then, by adding the girl we each Love into the worship, we would each experience a Love like never before. The triune was seen as three triangles. One of the angels reminded me of my friend Andrew. I wondered if it was him, or just an angel with similarities. This angel seemed nervous about the worship because he had never worshiped in the presence of friends before. After we worshiped, a car arrived at the front of the house. The house we were in was at the end of a cul-de-sac in a neighborhood with surrounding homes. An elder male angel stepped out of the car and said hello to me. He acted a little strange, and then his children got out and started running around. It was a magical moment. From my left, "the girl" arrived – though I thought it was from the same vehicle as the male angel's vehicle before me. She was almost naked, but covered where she would not be completely revealed in the eyes of others. She was as beautiful as always. When she stepped out of the vehicle something fell to the ground. I picked it up for her. I am sure she could sense my excitement. She stood in front of me as I stared mesmerized at her. For some inexplicable reason, I thought she would jump into my

Rebirth II

arms and give me a giant hug like two Lovers would do who had not seen each other for some time. As I write this, I can only laugh at my thoughts in that situation. But at the time, it felt very real. I placed my arms on either side of her and tried to help initiate her jumping into my arms. But, every time I tried, she remained rooted with one leg on the ground. I think she was actually trying to entertain me, but teach me a lesson at the same time. I became frustrated. I wanted to hug her so badly. She kept telling me that I would not be able to hold her "because you aren't trying." Eventually we parted ways, which left me feeling disappointed because I was not strong enough yet to hold an angel. I tried to rationalize that I could be strong enough if she had attempted to jump into my arms though instead of remaining rooted to the ground. Regardless, looking back on the moment as I write this, the thought that I could hold an angel of her stature makes me chuckle. As she walked away, another vehicle arrived from the left. Two baby girls hopped out of the car. It seemed like the children were mine, though I have no baseline as to why I would think that. I watched as they played loudly, full of Love. It was a beautiful moment. Those were the last images I saw as my soul returned to my body.

February 10, 2014

I arrived in the heavens this morning in a war-torn country that hated "my kind." There was a plantation house in the

The Written (cont'd)

jungle. A family lived there that was skeptical of me, though they allowed me into their home. I heard gunshots outside, and I was shown a horde of angry people. I was told to stay away. I eventually ran across Bryan in the house. He wanted me to remember all of the important parts of the conversation we shared earlier on Earth. That particular conversation was about looking for peace in the midst of whatever disruption caused the angel to become upset last night. I was thirsty and walked around the house in search of something to drink. I eventually found juice in the kitchen. After I drank the juice, I walked out of the house and attempted to journey across a field. The field felt thick and muddy beneath my feet – more so at the end so I could hardly free myself from the mud. I turned around and tried to find my way to a driveway so I could walk back to the house away from the mud. When I stepped out of the mud, I found a blade-less shovel (one of two tools on the ground) and began trying to scrape the mud off my shoe. I wondered if it was manure or mud. As I stood there I heard deep gunshots. I looked and saw a militia walking in formation on the adjacent property to the west. I ran into the house. When I neared the entrance one of the militia members pulled out a large, long barreled gun and took a shot at the house. I ran up the stairwells trying to avoid getting shot. I kept hearing someone telling me to get down. This same person continued to shout out that "the safe place is below." At the time, the words sounded literal (meaning I should duck for cover), but I also recognized the spiritual significance in the words. I continued running through the house and up a flight

Rebirth II

of stairs to avoid getting shot. I eventually decided the best course of action was to return to my body on Earth.

February 11, 2014

Last night I journeyed to a familiar house that is alongside a river. Every time I arrive at this house I wander over to the river and look for a boat. It seems like it would be a great piece of property to own because of the waterfront. But this time, I did not begin my adventure standing on the shoreline. I began inside a house. The house was full of what I could only call "wandering souls." These appeared to be souls that were in a state of trial or tribulation. Each one seemed as if they were aware where they were, but very lackadaisical about growing on their spiritual journey. Many were resting in chairs.

There was a large community room that most of us were in. One man carried on a conversation with me and propositioned me. I told him that I was straight, and that I would not indulge in his desires. He did not get bent out of shape. He seemed to take it in stride and responded, "Oh, that's cool. No worries." From that point I decided to head outside.

When I walked outside it was a cloudy day. I saw a house that I am more familiar with across the road (behind the house I was originally in). I decided to walk over to it. I wandered through the house looking for the angel that I generally have conversations with, but could not find him. I walked outside to the river and stood observing it. Just like every time in the past,

The Written (cont'd)

the river was raging ferociously in both its current and rapids. It is one of those rivers that looks deep with muddy water, but is white capped along the way. Each time I view the river, I realize no mechanical boat would be able to venture back upstream to the house if someone were to leave from there. It usually just makes me stop and ponder at the situation. This time was no different.

As I stood there, the angel appeared. He greeted me, and we stood there just watching the river. We chatted about it, no doubt rehashing the same conversations I have had in my past with him over the river. As the conversation drew to a close, he told me it was time to go, and I returned to my body.

After returning to my body, I decided to venture back to the heavens in search of resolve or guidance for my journey over the coming weeks. I am extremely excited about being able to give Lindsey my book and see the chain of events unfold. Most importantly, I am bursting at the seams in excitement of the potential for finding myself in the beginnings of a relationship with her. I want to be clear to acknowledge that while God has shared with me the path I am on, and the mile markers to strive toward, the outcome is completely in His control. All I can do is my best to hear the signs of what I need to do and keep gardening until the day arrives that we can meet at that coffee shop.

So, as I sought guidance, I found myself back in the heavens with a book in front of me. It was my book – the one I just finished (Gravity Calling). I was told to keep reading it – so I did, over and over. While I was in the heavens, I must have

Rebirth II

proofed it several times. Near the end, the book was pulled away from me, and I was allowed to see Lindsey and me together. This is where everything became fuzzy though.

While I observed us together for a significant period of time – and in everything I observed I saw us happy together, and we appeared to be in a relationship, I cannot recall any other detail. It is one of those occurrences that I am sure was shown to me in a way that I could try to find more resolve within, but not alter my journey forward. For if I knew the outcome in specifics, then free will would be encroached upon. So, I have to believe that what I was shown was just a haze of potential – and possibly resolve – to my nervous thoughts. And when I say nervous, it should be noted I mean anxious. The last part of the book discusses anxiety in depth, and I know that is a battle I am still fighting. This time, though, the battle is in the disguise of waiting for the destination.

For marathon runners know they have to run at least two hours to complete the race. Regardless how hard they run, two hours must pass to complete the race. The spiritual journey is no different. I often find myself running toward the destination as fast as I can, knowing that at a minimum I have eleven days before I receive the coffee mug with the key inside of it (part of the way I plan to deliver the book to Lindsey). And while that is perfect timing with Valentine's Day coming up in between, it is still hard on me. I know that I have at least this week to dance around a few text messages so that I can tell her I will not be at church this Sunday and to figure out which weekend she will be in town in the weeks following. These are the final

The Written (cont'd)

steps to putting the plan in motion. I will receive the book in print somewhere between the 14th and the 18th. The mug will be received by the 22nd. My daughter will be back in town either the weekend of the 23rd or March 2nd. I really want Lindsey to meet Georgia first and then setup the coffee meeting after – but that will have to be played by ear. I know the big marker on the calendar was to get through Valentine's Day first before anything happened, but pacing is something I struggle with.

Anyway, we will see how the timing remains to be played out. But as I sought peace in my trip to the heavens – and was likely shown peace through the experience – my earthly mind still reels at all of the potential. I have to continue stomping it out until I get to the destination.

February 12, 2014

My first experience in the heavens began with me stepping foot onto a location that I have only recently decided must be equivalent to the location mentioned in Dante's Inferno. The recent experiences of standing on the shore of a great rushing river, and also in seeing all of the lost souls has left me almost disheartened over the last few weeks. For every great experience, I feel like there has been reason for me to observe "the other side" of spiritual growth.

Bryan and I chatted about it in depth last night. That is when he decided to point me in the direction of Dante's Infer-

Rebirth II

no. I had never read it, nor did I know what it was about. But, I did find great similarities to the written descriptions of the torturous locations as described when Dante was standing with the Master. I have to believe there is a definite similarity in his literary work and my experiences. When he wrote the Divine Comedy, it was a time when people were suppressed from talking about spirituality outside of the bounds of common Catholic practices. Anything outside of the acceptable understanding of the spiritual world was subject to persecution. Many people disguised their experiences in art and through comedy and plays. So, this brings me back to my experience.

As I found myself standing in this location, I ran across one of the female souls I see frequently in this destination. We always share a conversation. This time, I decided I would explain to her that the experience she felt "trapped" in – and the same with me – was just a point of learning on the journey. I wanted her to know it was not real, and she had the ability to leave anytime she wanted. As I began explaining this concept to her, I could tell I had broken through the boundary of what was acceptable in the eyes of the negative energies there. Those beings maintained control through suppressing understanding and growth. By me sharing my awareness of where we were standing in the heavens, I began to jeopardize the very foundation the negative energies had built. I knew I had to speak quickly as I felt Lucifer approaching.

He came toward me, strong, with his minions as I kept explaining to the girl that she needed to get out of there. I wanted to save her – to help her. I continued telling her that

The Written (cont'd)

the hurt was necessary to see the light, but just a concept of the mind – not to be feared. As Lucifer approached, I was grabbed by the hand of God. His hand pulled me at the back of my neck (like a dog carries a puppy). He pulled me up from the land and pulled me over the great oceans of the deep. The oceans were rolling with seas of epic proportions. The land was a mountainous island in the middle of this raging ocean. I was meant to observe the location.

As I hovered over the oceans of the deep, Lucifer came toward me again. This time, God pulled me out from the oceans and into another location. Lucifer continued to try to appear before me, filling my mind with his face, but God would not allow it. He filled the location with blinding light causing the darkness of Lucifer to be pushed out of the area we were in. I was allowed to rest in this location momentarily and understand what all I had observed, and then my spirit was allowed to return to my body.

While I am not sure if this means that my experiences of learning in this Inferno land have drawn to a close, for now I have peace in knowing that part of this experience was intended for me to help save lost souls with the strength of God watching over me. It was to understand that I have a new set of standards I must abide by. For God has shown me so many great things that I now have a higher set of guidelines from which never to stray. Observing this land was also partly to help me understand the ramifications for not continuing to progress. It is a stalled place on the journey I would never

Rebirth II

want to experience again, much less find myself stuck from choosing not acknowledge my King's great Love for me.

After returning to my body, I journaled the experience and returned to the heavens. This time I found myself in a great hall or library. It was made of alabaster. There were two specific angels that were the gatekeepers of this particular area. One continued shuffling through paperwork and scrolls, eventually finding a set of scrolls needed. It seemed like what I was observing was at the very least a metaphorical explanation of priming my spirit to travel to other locations.

One angel stuffed the scrolls into a container that I was told was a "soul." The papers barely fit and were folded and bent in order for the container to be closed. It was at this point I felt like my heavenly body and soul were split and I was able to experience either's perspective. I flipped between being the "container" and the observer. Eventually the two dualities became one as I found myself floating on my back where the container was with the angel. It was very relaxing. He pulled me into some sort of a machine with pillars that created a great light. As it lit up in great light, I felt as if I was receiving some sort of a spiritual upgrade – for lack of a better way of explaining it. As the light became brighter, I eventually flashed out of the location and returned to my body. While I cannot be sure whether what I experienced was metaphorical or tangible, the concept remains that after experiencing the Inferno, I had taken steps forward to the next starting line that would be set before me.

The Written (cont'd)

The final experience was a shared experience with Bryan. As I would come to find out in a conversation with him the following day, He is getting engaged this upcoming weekend, and I am supposed to help him out with his proposal. While I have never seen the location we are going to be on Saturday, Bryan and I were allowed to journey forward in time to observe the events that would happen on this upcoming Saturday. When we chatted about it, we filled in each other's sentences acknowledging we were both there. I explained the location in detail, though I have never seen it. He explained the clothes I was wearing and other smaller details that I was keenly aware of from my perspective. I explained the same types of details to him. Overall, we witnessed the preceding five to ten minutes leading up to the moment of his proposal. Neither of us observed the outcome, but we definitely experienced the events prior.

February 13, 2014

There is not much to write about from this morning's experience. I was extremely tired when I went to bed from a heavy workout routine. So, while I did traverse the heavens, I would say my travels were clumsy at best. I did not maintain a great harmony and would continue to fall in and out of harmony with the locations. One particular moment that was impressed upon me was in witnessing an extremely obese lost soul. I was supposed to watch her and her actions. She at-

Rebirth II

tempted to lure me into her "lair" (if you could call it that). She was extremely filthy and exuded an overall disgusting feeling. Her appearance was almost in a melted state versus the more human-like features I typically see. She wanted to consume my body in any way she could – sexually, nibbling, biting. She was very primal and carnal. After just a few minutes of trying to figure out what it was I was supposed to learn from the experience, I decided to leave the lair. I could not take the exposure to the filth any more. Even upon leaving I felt scarred somehow for even having to observe the experience.

February 14, 2014

While I would Love to explain everything that occurred in the heavens this morning, the best I can offer is that I read a lot…..I mean A LOT. When I arrived in the heavens, a book was placed before me that seemed to have an unending number of pages for me to read. So, I read. Often, reading words in the heavens is difficult to do. Words seem to be illegible or in a constant state of flux. I can only imagine it is what it must feel like as a child learns to read for the first time. Those childhood memories are generally long lost as a child grows up, but during those first years, reading is difficult. So just like on Earth, reading in the heavens is tantamount to learning to read a divine language with no formal instructions. Though to the mind, the words eventually are understood in a native, in-

The Written (cont'd)

tuitive way (often appearing in your native tongue when words are understood), the process of getting there is difficult.

I find I read a lot in the heavens. I can only assume my soul absorbs the knowledge and it becomes applicable in my earthly walk, but I rarely can recount the words I read. This morning's experience was no different. I spent hours upon hours of speed-reading in this great book. The words all made sense as I read. I even re-explored concepts on earlier pages and flipped through the book to re-read points of reference. But – in this moment – I could not begin to explain one thing I read in this voyage to the heavens. So, as uneventful as this entry may seem, it was actually quite a deep and mesmerizing experience for the duration I was there.

February 17, 2014

During meditation my spirit was calmed by the angels in the heavens. But near the end, the man in rose-colored glasses came at me trying to add doubt to the questions that the angels were granting me peace about. They quickly pulled me into another location where he could not follow. It was during this time I heard his voice echo those same words he tried to speak to me several weeks prior, "She's not the one for you…" But when my soul returned to my body, I actually felt stronger – more resilient in my confidence for the angels had granted me peace.

Rebirth II

February 18, 2014

During the last several days, I have not written much about my journeys to the heavens. Over the course of the last few weeks I have been exhausting my body with daily workout routines which cause the experiences to be harder to bring back with me even though I have continued to have experiences in the heavens. But, the more important point I want to make is that I have willfully chosen to not write them down.

The last couple of months has been a surge of spiritual activity in my life, and now that I am in the final leg of a race into the Promised Land, I have been trying to maintain my spiritual center and focus on the destination during the last few weeks, and some of the experiences (such as the Inferno) have been stressful to my soul. Though I know God has a purpose and intention in showing me these places, I realized they have been introducing doubt in my mind and my spiritual center. And while I know fear and doubt is not His intention, I knew that I was close to unraveling if I could not find peace.

I prayed for His help wherein He pulled me from the Inferno. After that night, I have had only the warmest and peaceful experiences in the Heavens. The experiences have returned to locations of familiarity – ones with the angels I have come to know along the journey. And while I am not sure if the experiences in the Inferno are over, I know that once I came to an understanding of that particular location in the heavens, I did try to save people – which is when Lucifer

The Written (cont'd)

chased me, and God protected me. So I say all of that to say that the experiences following have been welcomed experiences to my mind and soul. Many of the nights, mornings, or meditations I would return to my body and just lie in bed contemplating each experience. For me, I did not need to write them down as this was a period of "recovery" for me. But, I realize the purpose is not just for me, but the words I will leave behind. So, I will make a better effort at ensuring I write down every experience as it happens.

With that said, this morning I experienced a type of spiritual training in the heavens. This training was targeted at building my faith without sight. As has occurred in the recent experiences I have not written about, the environment was hard to observe in definition due to a blanket of snow that had covered the ground.

Periodically, snow will fall in the experiences. I have taken this as a type of communication from God. In my recent observation, it seems that snow is "God's confetti" falling down around us. But this experience was different. This experience placed me in the midst of a blizzard of epic proportions. Each part of the training consisted of me having to navigate a short distance in the blizzard. Eventually, I took a vehicle into the blizzard and on the interstate. I had to face the blizzard by myself (which was important). I could not see three feet in front of me and was driving on blind faith. Everything around me was in a vicious snowstorm, blanketed in white.

Eventually I realized I would not be able to drive the vehicle without endangering others, so I stepped out of it. I

Rebirth II

wondered if I should build an igloo in the middle of the road to keep the wind out, but decided that was equally a poor idea since someone else may drive down the road. I eventually realized I had to follow God's voice through the blizzard. I took several steps to my left and felt the snow crunch beneath my feet. The sound was different though – it was not the same type of snow that surrounded me. I quickly realized that the texture of the snow beneath my feet was a type of spiritual recognition in following the right path – the path that God wanted me to follow. Whether the snow was really a different texture or not was irrelevant because it was the spiritual recognition that was important.

    I began to wander in the blizzard, un-fearing of the weather or of danger. I knew the next steps were to just follow where I recognized He was leading me. As I wandered, I suddenly heard a couple of giggles and a voice shout out, "Over here. This way!" The voice came from one of two angels I see regularly in my experiences, though it has been several weeks since we saw each other. These are two extremely beautiful female angels – faces of porcelain.

    I hurried over in their direction. They told me to move quickly – to hurry. I did as best as I could. They stayed behind me as we ran through the blizzard. They constantly called out directions for me to take. They continued to tell me to run faster. It was as if my best efforts at running were not quick enough for wherever we were going – but I tried. Eventually they shouted to me, "Quick! A train is coming!! In here!!" We

The Written (cont'd)

headed into a tunnel dimly lighted. They continued to shout at me to run faster, that the train was going to hit me.

I ran as fast as I could. I never turned around because I was not sure if the train was that close, or if it was even relevant. Seeing it would do nothing but distract me, I kept running. Just as we made it out of the tunnel, the angels veered to the right, and I jumped to the left. Right then a train came rolling through the tunnel behind us. It missed hitting us by inches. I smiled at them.

Though we were separated by the train, we transported to a place together. I am not quite sure how it happened, but it seemed natural in the motion – as if the train dividing us did not really exist. As I stared at them, they continued to giggle. They were clearly entertained by me. As we were running, they giggled as well – but I was too focused on the destination to pay much attention at that time. So as we sat there, I marveled at their appearance.

Seeing these two particular angels is always a huge moment. I can tell they hold great importance in the heavens, but I always hesitate to place names on either of them. I fully believe one of them is Arielle – the other one is possibly Anael. But, again, I am not sure. These two angels appeared to me early on in my dreams and visions. They are almost mother figures to me in how they have been a part of teaching me all I have learned. But even though I say they are motherly, their age is timeless and radiate beauty. They are stunning.

These two angels are both blonde with fair skin. Their eyebrows are both very defined. This time, I studied one of

Rebirth II

their faces just soaking in the details. This is the first time I took notice to the complexities of their eyebrows. The one I observed had to have known I was just soaking it in. She just allowed me to stare, smiling back at me. Her eyebrows followed the geometry of a Fibonacci spiral, but more subtle in definition. Where the eyebrow begins near the center of the forehead, the individual hairs spiraled in that particular ratio before spanning out in the arc of the brow.

Now while I describe the eyebrow as geometric in shape, in visual appearance, it would not appear like that at first glance – only in detailed observance of how the hair lay directionally did it become apparent. This little detail resonated deep within me. Their eyes were mesmerizing with a clear definition of eyeliner. They were stoic, beautiful and perfect in every way I could ever imagine a perfect face could be – but they were both different. Their faces were like porcelain. It was a conundrum, because they each represented perfection, though they were distinctly different.

As I observed the angels sitting before me, suddenly a small dog appeared between them. It was black and gray with curly hair. It was unlike any dog I have seen on Earth. It was similar to a Maltee-Poo, but slightly bigger. It was cute and playful. The angels just continued to giggle. I suppose the overwhelming number of details I was observing and just the very moment of standing in the presence of great angels must have caused me to lose harmony, because I found myself flying back to my body where I awoke to write down the experience.

The Written (cont'd)

While I know there will be more to be gleaned from the experience, my immediate take-away was that the world around me may seem cloudy at times – impossible to see direction – but I must have faith in God. And in that faith, the angels will help guide me and show me the path to follow. I had several additional experiences after the event with the angels, but again, I did not write them down. Each one was so vivid in my memory that I thought I would be able to write about the experience at a later point in the day – but alas, I cannot recall the details. I do know that each experience continued to fill me with resolve in my spiritual actions and efforts on my journey.

February 19, 2014
Early Morning

I found myself on the ice for a hockey game. It was the same rink that I practiced on in previous visions. This time, though, it was a full game scenario. It had to have been near the end of the game because before the face-off, two separate timeouts were called by the opposing team (the second one was a twenty-second timeout). I was playing defense. As I stood back to defend an open-net goal, I was covering one of the opposing players. I knew their game plan was to give this guy the puck after the face-off, which meant I would be the targeted defenseman.

Rebirth II

After the timeouts, the puck dropped and it was kicked over to the guy I was guarding. I did all I could to prevent his shot on the goal – and I think I deflected it because the puck squirted by me in slow motion toward the open-netted goal. I assume our goalie had been pulled because we needed an extra player to score a point to tie the game. The shot on the goal skirted to the left of the goal post, missing by only inches. I skated over to it and circled behind the net. I was very fluid on my skates – a fluidity I had not experienced in the other visions that involved hockey. In fact, I have never played hockey nor ice-skated other than one time on a date, so the hockey scenario is never one I would have picked. But, it was apparent this was part of my spiritual journey for some reason.

I took the puck and skated toward the other goal. I was excited because I knew I was demonstrating a quality to my hockey skills in saving the goal and getting the puck. As I skated, I heard one teammate skating behind me telling me to drop it to him. There was another teammate looping around the goal and flying into an opening on the left side of the rink. I dropped the puck and backed up to center ice. The teammate I dropped the puck to passed it to the guy flying open on the left, where he took a shot. He missed, but we recovered and the game continued.

At some point in the height of the excitement, I lost harmony with the moment and returned to my body. I was left with several questions that honestly have no answers at this point. Those questions all revolve around the reason of the experience. Possibly it is just a way for me to increase my spir-

The Written (cont'd)

itual growth in the equivalent of athleticism. But I am curious if I may have at some point in the past (or the future) been a hockey player in another life. I am also curious why many of my recent experiences in the heavens involve ice and snow. I wonder if my body is overheating more often and the scenario needs to be colder – or it could be the opposite. Am I overheating because the scenario is colder in sensation? I suppose it is possible that the cold experiences are all to build my spiritual strength and stature for longer experiences since the biggest component in maintaining harmony seems in regulating earthly body temperature when the soul leaves the body.

After I returned to my body, I cooled down and jaunted back to the heavens. This time I was sitting in a classroom. I watched as a book flew over the heads of the students from the back of the classroom to the front. It moved gracefully – without gravity interfering. There was a group of three or four students up front who treated the book like a soccer ball. It was as if they were actually playing a soccer game with the book serving as the ball.

As the book approached one of the defenders, an attacker went to kick the book but collided legs with the defender who reached it just prior to the attacker did, in order to clear it out. It is also important to note that the students all seemed to be flying, but I could not see any discernible wings. I did have the impression there were wings on each student, I just could not see them clearly. So, as the book hurtled across the students' heads in the direction of the back of the room, it headed in the direction of an open cabinet. As it reached the bottom right

Rebirth II

corner (which was elevated similar to a kitchen cabinet over the counter), a man shut the door trapping the book's cover and a few pages between the corner and the doorway. The remainder of the book was flapping below. I could see the book was the book I had just finished writing – Gravity Calling.

A boy walked up to the book and said, "Cool." Suddenly there was a magic sound – like the sound of chimes and swirling particle effects. It seemed as if it could have been a commercial for something like iBooks. The purpose that I could glean was that the book held within it the potential to spark the imaginations of others. Only when the book stopped moving, could it be observed that the emotions that were rushing through the room were the imaginations of the children, fueled by the words bound within the book.

Each of the previous two experiences lasted a great deal of time. The hockey game seemed to last longer. But I ended up having a third experience that was more of a wobbly, flux-like experience without form. It seemed like I was just a ball of consciousness. I wish I could say definitively that I was standing in the presence of God, but it is hard to say. The only other times I have had this type of experience have been in His presence where He wanted to impart knowledge to me. These are the toughest experiences to bring back to Earth because there are no words that can describe the sensations and feelings of being a ball of consciousness that is being taught concepts through the language of God. But with that said, I

The Written (cont'd)

cannot say definitively this time that I was in the presence of God, but I have to believe that is the situation.

The experience was filled with blinding light all around me. The concepts being relayed to me all dealt with Love and strength. I continued to see the outline of a heart form and burst into light. It began at the point at the base, and each side was traced simultaneously – indicating two souls in motion. Each outline of the heart took a fluid, curvy motion that had an extra curl added to the outline. But when the two glowing ends of the outlines finished the shape of the heart and met in the top middle, a blinding light was created. It was then that the outlined heart would spin in three-dimensional space for a few minutes as it would disappear and begin again.

I was brought back to my body by my alarm clock going off, but I opened my eyes with an overwhelming feeling of warmth and Love. It was as if God was trying to show me that two souls would become one. I am sure it had to do with strength in the situation with Lindsey – to calm my nerves. But for every bit of calm it adds, I get that much more eager to be at the finish line already.

February 19, 2014
Mid-Morning

Though I usually reserve this book for journal entries alone, I want to also add an entry about two special moments between God and me that occurred over the last few days.

Rebirth II

One event occurred the previous day. The other this morning. Over the last several days I have been praying incessantly for God to grant me peace while waiting for March 15th to roll around. That is the day that He has told me would be the day Lindsey and I should meet up at the coffee shop for me to give her the book. If the events leading into the book seem unbelievable, and even the context of the book itself seem improbable – just imagine being me for a moment and having faith that this seemingly unbelievable event is actually in motion. It is the hardest part of my journey to date. In the beginning, I had nothing to lose, so all I had to do was have faith that I was moving forward in the right direction. Now, my heart has been exposed in a way that I have never experienced before in my entire life. I can say that without any reservations. In everything I thought I had with Stacey, it still pales in comparison to how I feel in this moment with Lindsey…and we have not even seen each other outside of church.

My heart is delicate – quite possibly the single greatest part of vulnerability my soul has remaining. This is most definitely why this portion of the journey has to come after the growth in the other areas – because the foundation has to be built to handle this level of faith. Nothing is greater than Love. It can wreck a person to the core, or fuel the soul for eternity. For me, I was crushed by a failed marriage and have taken the journey to the point I am at right now. I am standing in the midst of something that seems impossible – but is clearly being held in God's hands. It is a moment that I cannot do anything but feel humbled and unworthy of all it is to become. I will

The Written (cont'd)

always feel like the breath of amazing that God has shared with me is a breath that I could just have easily have never received from Him when I fell off the tracks of my spiritual growth. But anyway – I do not want to snowball my thoughts in that particular area right now. For now, I want to share the events of the previous two days.

So since every bit of the plan has gone into action with March 15th as the focus date for Lindsey, I have found myself in prayer nearly every chance I get. I have found that the only way to deal with my emotions during the space between now and then is to turn to Him and show him the most reverence I can and let Him know I see His hand at work.

Yesterday, my prayer consisted of me thanking Him for everything and asking Him to help me understand what I am supposed to do. I am "all in" spiritually and financially. Both of these firsts are new for me after I went "all in" during my first marriage and my subsequent business venture that eventually led to my Genesis. All I could do was tell God that I am naked, exposed and vulnerable to His will. And though I know His intentions, I did not want to misstep. If I was supposed to be sending text messages or reaching out to Lindsey, I wanted to do it. But I found myself just asking God for guidance. I knew that He was holding me, so I just wanted to let it be His will. His timing is immaculate after all.

I just had so much unrest as to whether I should even be texting Lindsey. That was the focal point of the prayer for the last half, pleading to Him. As the prayer was coming to an end, I received a text message. I ignored it, and told God that I

Rebirth II

would wait for His guidance to check the message if He was attempting to communicate with me. So after the third buzz, I recognized that God was again reaching out to me in a now familiar way. I checked my phone to find a tweet flashing on my screen from a friend. It said, "Best convo ever. #silence." All I could do was smile. Somehow, in light of every means of communication possible I had asked Him whether I should be actionable in texting Lindsey or whether I should remain silent and wait on Him. Those were literally my words to Him...and He answered with precision. I could not do much else but thank Him for answering me while weeping in humility in the moment of hearing His voice.

So as I started the following day with resolve to not text Lindsey while I let silence hold the conversation of our souls without words, I continued to find strength in God's words. In every way He has communicated to me, I have listened – and this time would be no different. We have not texted in over a week, though she did favorite my tweet on Valentine's Day (a not-so-subtle call out to her feelings and intentions.) It was her first favorite on Twitter of mine since we started seeing each other in church. By the end of the day, I was again feeling unrest in the wait until the 15th. At lunch and later on in the evening I turned to God in prayer to help find resolve. While I was no longer questioning the 15th or even the possibility of His actions, I needed an ear to hear me talk.

I prayed for quite a while and, after much rambling, found myself asking for only one thing in the prayer – but even then retracting it at the end. As I neared the end of my prayer,

The Written (cont'd)

I asked Him if there was a way for me to know He was working in her life the same way He is working in mine... in knowing that, it would help grant me peace. I added in my conversation that I believed He was working in her life, and that I had no question about it – I just wished there was a way of me knowing. Possibly we could have an experience in the heavens with our souls – but then I comically added that particular concept may be "cheating" as I had to grow spiritually in learning to deal with the wait. I ended the prayer acknowledging that I was asking Him for nothing because I just had to have faith that He was holding us both in His hands. I asked for forgiveness for my errant, rambling thoughts, but thanked Him for listening to me.

Now let's rewind to yesterday for the other experience. When I awoke from my experience in the heavens with the hockey game, I journaled it by putting notes into my phone. When I reached for my phone, I had a tweet notification from Lindsey. It was not directed to me – just a normal tweet. I looked at it and couldn't help but feel the overwhelming nature of God's hand. At 11:11 p.m., she posted a picture of an open chocolate wrapper that had the words "Love Every Moment" printed inside of it. Lindsey's tweet was captioned with the words, "Life is so strange sometimes. It reminded me to go with it. Can't argue with chocolate."

Now – at the surface level it may not seem that big. But several things which happened in that tweet were undeniably the hand of God offering me reassurance in His work in Lindsey's life. Whether she was hearing His words or not should

Rebirth II

not be my concern. This tweet was for me to see His work. For starters, it was posted at 11:11 p.m. This is a time that people "make a wish" for it being a lucky number. In fact, I have made sure to send several texts to Lindsey at 11:11 (a.m. or p.m. depending on the conversation point). And while I suppose it could be possible we are making different wishes at those times, God let me know we were wishing on the same outcome.

The second major point was that she listened to the words from a chocolate wrapper. The concept of chocolate is so dominant in my book and the chapters regarding Lindsey that there could not be another way to more overtly shout-out the work of His divine hand. God had sent me on a mission to get chocolate for Lindsey before we ever met – and though I never told her it was from me, it was the recognition in the series of actions that were obvious here.

The third – and most bluntly placed sign – was that she posted a message about Love. She has avoided all concepts of Love prior to Valentine's Day in the wake of her last relationship ending. God did not just deliver a message that involved one item that could be taken out of context, He signed it with three signatures. Again, I want to emphasize – whether Lindsey knows what is coming or not should not be my concern (though I do hope she is wishing our souls will collide again as much as I am longing for them to do so). While the scenario may not be quite like this, it makes me smile to think of the possibility that she was wishing on me at 11:11, and posted that message so I would see.

The Written (cont'd)

After I saw the message, I prayed thanks to God and wept for what must have been thirty minutes. I even joked about what a crier I have become, and how I have no idea how to handle the abundance of emotions that have been pouring out of me recently. The tears do not happen in my earthly walk – only through His divine actions. And, it is not crying – it's weeping. I suppose tears are tears when they come from a man, but if it means that I recognize how God is working in my life, then these are tears I want to experience every day the rest of my life.

February 22, 2014

When I arrived in the heavens, I found myself standing in an apartment building of a downtown metropolitan area. A man who had been shot came over and spoke with me. As it turned out, the bullet that wounded this person came from the barrel of a gun owned by someone named Matt. As I stood there, a beautiful blonde angel came to me. She was beautiful and is one of the angels I see regularly in my travels. She is the angel that reminds me of a friend named Brittany (but only in facial characteristics). This angel wanted to take me over and introduce me to another angel named "Candace" whom I had not yet met.

The angel led me to a residence where we all gathered around a table for dinner. Candace was at the table, as well as other angels I did not know. Candace was beautiful as well.

Rebirth II

We all had dinner and carried on great conversation. Though I felt like a child when I realized I was drawing a picture at the table, the angels did not see it as such. I drew something that showed the progression of two people falling in Love. The angels showed a lot of interest in my drawing and spoke praises about it among themselves. There were a lot of words and phrases spoken by the angels that I did not understand, but everyone was happy to see me.

February 23, 2014

The experience in the heavens this morning again involved Lindsey. It began with me meeting Lindsey's soul at church. When I entered into the church, the service was just starting. I was greeted by angels who seemed very glad to see me. The lights were dim. Lindsey knew I was coming, but that is all. She knew nothing of my feelings toward her.

The service was packed. I observed extremely tall angels throughout the church. Before I was taken to my seat, the angelic hostess told me to "take off my coat because it was making too much noise." We laughed about it. Suddenly another hostess appeared. She said, "She's this way." In my excitement, I did not follow. I wanted to lead. But by leading, I could not see where they were telling me to go. When I turned around for help, one angel came and said, "She moved. She was just there. Now she is not. She is sitting up on the right hand side now."

The Written (cont'd)

I walked back through the lobby of the church and observed several families. I was hoping to see Lindsey waiting for me. I entered back through the right side this time and saw where seats had recently become empty. I assumed she had been sitting there too for a brief moment. I walked to the front of the sanctuary looking for her. I stopped and realized she was not to be found. I walked back feeling rejected. As I headed back up the aisle, I heard an angel again say, "She's over here." as her words were interrupted and tailed off in the ending of the sentence.

The interjecting sentence was, "No. He needs to see this." It was as if everyone in the sanctuary was aware of my specific situation, and they were all playing roles in my lesson. I walked up the aisle. I walked up a couple of stairs to my right to find a seat in the upper section of the sanctuary. I passed a boy running. I thought it may be Lindsey's son, but I did not want to see with my eyes because I already felt rejected. Though I did not make eye contact with the boy, he said, "She's here."

He turned and ran up to where she was sitting. I did not turn to look. I pretended I did not see her. As I went to find a seat, several angels slid down the pew and let me sit down next to them. The room was in darkness bathed in blue and purple light. The male angel that moved down asked if I was okay. I said I was, though I felt rejected. I turned toward the front hoping Lindsey would come find me instead of me seeking her because I knew it would appear I was trying too hard.

I returned to my body, took notes, and returned to the heavens. I passed a "latch keeper" as I took a right along a

Rebirth II

road in a divided and open field. The latch keeper made wax seals and bezels. In earthly terms, I have never heard the term "latch keeper" but that is the term that was shared with me as to this angel's role. I finally was able to reach him but lost harmony when I debated on what to ask him before I was to run down the road.

    I returned once again to the heavens. When I returned, I was shown a series of gold items that I was responsible for. We stood on a platform in the middle of a barren land. I stood before a great angel who seemed to be responsible for the oversight of this platform. He told me they normally would not allow for me (or as I better understood it, a human's soul in the heavens) to use the particular kind of transportation I was attempting to use. It seemed there was supposed to be a train arriving behind the angel.

    A voice boomed over my shoulder. "Is that all you have?" the voice asked. It was an austere, elder angel. I said it was. He said, "Okay then. We normally don't do this, but in your circumstance, it will be just fine." He then shouted out several names, including my earthly name, "Jonathan." The angel let out one final shout, "All Aboard!" We stepped into our places along the platform, lined up with the train tracks. The angel said, "We will be departing in T minus three hours." I was confused as I tried to rationalize the absurdity of the math and returned to my body.

The Written (cont'd)

February 25, 2014

This morning's experience in the heavens was extremely vivid. Unfortunately, I took very few notes and forgot to expand upon my notes quickly enough to fill in all of the lush detail. The gist of the first of the two experiences was that I was in a piano shop. The shopkeeper (an angel) wanted me to see all of the pianos. He walked me around and over to each piano. While I would try to play a song on one of the pianos, the mechanism for the keys did not function in the way I am used to on Earth. It seemed to express a higher level of mathematics in the notes.

I saw another instrument that resembled a harpsichord. The shopkeeper gave me something with the text "V23-11 EX." I was unsure what it meant, but assumed it must correspond to a harmonic frequency or a Bible verse I needed to reference. The shopkeeper also told me that Bryan had just been there earlier, and he had given Bryan something to take as well. He emphasized that I saw the intricacies of how everything worked and how they fit into the big picture. Then he explained that Bryan saw the big picture and understood how the intricacies worked within. It was implied that this was one of the reasons that Bryan and I are spiritual brethren.

I returned to Earth and journaled the experience. I returned to the heavens to see a blonde angel with a potter. The angel was celebrating my effort of including a key within the clay mug that I planned to give Lindsey. Both the angel and

Rebirth II

the potter were very proud in the symbolism I was led to use in my efforts with Lindsey.

March 3, 2014

This morning's travels to the heavens began on the football field. I played the position of quarterback. At one point I had to scramble and score a touchdown. The team was excited for me. On another play, I was a receiver, and a ball was hurled at me as I stood in the end zone. I missed the catch even though it was thrown right to me. My teammates explained to me what I did wrong, though they did not seem upset. It was an opportunity for me to learn. I was wide open, which was the disappointing part of the experience. After the football game, we all went to a soccer field. The goals were offset from each other. During the second and fourth periods (of five), the teams played on a shortened field. The fifth period (which was the center period) was played in the style of a hybrid version of tennis and soccer. I lost harmony and returned to my body.

When I returned to the heavens, I arrived on a train with three other angels. We were all going to Vegas to celebrate some accomplishment. It was a much more advanced future world than we have today on Earth.

Upon returning to my body, I prayed. After my prayer, I returned once again to the heavens. A female angel began speaking to me while the spirit of Lindsey and one of her girl

The Written (cont'd)

friends walked in. The female angel was frustrated that I had become distracted. We were all about to board an airplane. As everyone was boarding, I felt like I was hurting myself having not talked to Lindsey yet. The angel tried to avert my attention and called me over to a staircase. We stood beneath the staircase as she spoke to me directly. She told me to focus on her (the angel) and to not "read into" or "look at" Lindsey. I was further told not to pay any attention to Lindsey's actions in my life.

I apologized to the angel for being distracted. My distraction prevented us from having the conversation the angel wanted to have with me. She had a glowing orb – or something that resembled an earring – in her left ear. It was unlike anything I had seen before. The angel gave me a big hug. I took notice of her beauty. She had a long flowing white dress. I asked her if we could try this again sometime (indicating meeting up with her and carrying on the conversation). She just smiled, but did not reply. I understood her words to be a direct answer to a prayer just prior to the vision where I vented to God about being unable to focus because Lindsey's actions continued to pull me out of focus from having unbridled faith in the destination.

The angel had told me to focus on her – meaning, have faith and not be distracted by any of the noise created from others or Lindsey along the way. I also took it to mean that Lindsey may not "see me" yet, but will upon everything working out. As I was boarding the plane, I realized I forgot my bag. I ran down the stairs and into the building. It looked

Rebirth II

more like a supermarket than a flight concourse. I eventually found my way to a familiar place where the motherly angel ("the girl") was standing. I spoke with her. I asked if she was coming with us – and told her that we were about to leave. She smiled at me and told me she would be there – to not worry about her. She also emphasized for me to "stay focused." Suddenly, the vision switched to me driving a car and looking off to the right. I was distracted. I glanced to my right and then looked back straight ahead to see traffic at a standstill because of a wreck. I flew at a high rate of speed into the wreck. I can only assume I crashed quite hard. That is when I awoke. Essentially, I was told by the angel in a metaphor to "look straight ahead and not allow myself to be distracted."

After the vision, I prayed to God acknowledging I heard His message. Afterwards, I closed my eyes and found myself observing a pit of lions. The lions appeared to be without manes. An angel was placing bloody meat in a large tray that wrapped around the cage. After he dumped the meat into the tray, he pushed it through the black iron gate. We were standing above the top of a stone cave that appeared unreachable by the lions. The lions were all relaxing down below. The angel looked at me and explained something very important – but it was without words, which will make this harder for me to write about.

He impressed upon me that the lions were fed a hearty meal, but while people observed them, the lions would not feed on the meat. He also explained something about the pride of the lion causing them to want to make the kill themselves.

The Written (cont'd)

This pride prevented them from ever being satisfied with being fed. He then showed me how, when the lights went out in the early morning hours of night and no one was around, the rare lion will climb onto the cave structure and feed on the delicacies placed before him. The illustration showed the lion separating itself from the other lions and removing his own pride from the pride in order to feed on all that had been prepared for him. It was emphasized that this lion was rare – and that it did not even allow the other lions to see its actions. It kept its actions hidden in the night when there were no observers. There were other thoughts impressed to me, but it was extremely hard to decipher the words because the communication was through archetypal concepts.

March 4, 2014

I travelled to the heavens but could not return with anything beyond a vague setting of a house.

March 5, 2014

This morning, I arrived in a house in the heavens. I was being hidden away from the others and helped to escape from something unknown. I was being chased by a blue/gray-skinned race. They wanted me captured. The house I found myself in was familiar. It was the same house and scenario as yesterday – but yesterday I could not escape, nor could I recall

Rebirth II

the experience with enough clarity to return to Earth with it. Every time I got close to escaping, I was caught. This time, I escaped out of a window and ran as fast as I could. The other race's weapons were flaming arrows. They shot at me, but missed. They also used sharpened sticks as weapons. When I ran, I ran faster than any of them. Eventually, I was joined by another angel. We ran together. The angel helped me escape. It took both of us to act as a distraction to the chasers in order for us to escape their pursuit. When we knew we were safe, I turned to see one of our chasers standing upon a tall ledge that he was using as a lookout post. With one final attempt, he shot at us, but intentionally missed. We made brief eye contact, and I acknowledged he missed on purpose. He turned and ran. At this point, the angel looked at me in the face. I noticed she had arrow markings drawn in the inner corners of her eyes. They glistened. They were a darker tone to the color of her skin. She reminded me of Neytiri from Avatar, but was distinctly different in race and form.

March 7, 2014

I arrived in the heavens riding in the rear of a train. I was looking out the window when a man ran up with a girl. He was trying to get her onboard but needed my help. When we made eye contact, he asked me directly to help. He pushed her up and into my arms, but I was not strong enough to hold her. She hung on, and he helped by pushing her up and onto the

The Written (cont'd)

train. I stood there, saddened, realizing I could not help as much as he wanted me to. The girl could have represented Lindsey, and the man, God, who was trying to help us work out. But in symbolism, it was clear He was telling me there is a handoff occurring wherein I needed to help her get to the destination with me. The train was symbolic of the spirit and allowing God to carry us through. The big takeaway from the vision was on the handoff and the apparent need for me to try to help despite how inconsequential my efforts may be compared to God's helping hand. It may even be a direct message telling me I am not strong enough to hold onto her yet (spiritually). The message was deeply rooted and could transcend to many other aspects of life. But, I am able to recognize at least one of the earthly representations. And, just as everything God reveals occurs with multiple meanings, this one was no different. To take it one step further, if Lindsey represents "the girl" who represents Love, then on an even more primal level, God was saying that I was not strong enough to Love the way he desires for me (with Lindsey or any other person). He also showed that even at my strongest, He would still have to help bring us together as well.

March 8, 2014

While the experience was brief, I was standing before a train. The train was about to depart and I had to board it. I

Rebirth II

cannot recount anymore than this part of the experience. The rest seems just like hazy details at this point.

March 10, 2014
Early Morning

 The first experience in the heavens this morning consisted of me performing my daily earthly routine. This is fairly typical when my body and mind are not properly aligned to experience the heavens. My mind runs through earthly routines as if on autopilot. It takes a nudge or a gentle reminder to realize where I am, and then the experience can begin to take place. Sometimes I think of this place as a "limboland" – like a concourse where souls are waiting for their flight.

 Often, the whirlwind type of moment when the soul is taken to the heavens manifests in a way that the mind rationalizes as something with movement. This can be a train, a plane, a boat, but most often it comes in the form of a tornado or vortex. In actuality, the tornado is probably the most appropriate communication of the method of transport because moving between the heavens and the Earth occurs in a Fibonacci-esque like movement; a polarized spinning across the spheres that comprise existence. And while most will not at first see the symbolism in the movie I am about to mention, the very illustration of the tornado in both The Wizard of Oz and Oz, The Great & Powerful are meant to replicate this exact scenario. The land of Oz is even more appropriately

The Written (cont'd)

defined in the more recent movie. Listen to the words, the context. It becomes quite clear that the world that the Wizard is experiencing is a representation of the Heavens where the Good Witch is a great angel helping him all along to find Love.

In the midst of my enactment of my earthly routines, I became aware of a tornado rolling through the parking lot where I was parking my Jeep. The moment became real for me. I became aware that I was driving around an angel. Probably a better explanation is that an angel was present with me awaiting for me to spiritually awaken – sort of like an angelic babysitter. When this occurred, we parked and we both got out of the car quickly. It was important to not be swept up by the tornado this time – the reason is that it would be the return path from the heavenly world I was in, back to my body. We both leapt behind a wall to brace for the tornado to roll through. As I began to realize we would be safe where we were hiding, I felt the need to peer over the wall. When I stood up and looked, I was sucked up by the tornado and returned to my body.

While I had several other experiences in the heavens, I cannot recount any other, save for the last one…which was an answer to a prayer earlier in the evening. Over the preceding weeks, my workout routine has continued to exhaust my body. And while I know that it is affecting my spiritual travels, there is also an earthly importance (at least for the next several weeks) to be in the best muscular shape of my life. I do not want this to sound shallow, because I know that is the potential

Rebirth II

of what I am writing, but it is important that when Lindsey and I meet at the beach on the weekend of the 28th, that everything be as ideal as possible. This means the journey there, every event that occurs at the resort, every detail that can be polished should be done with the utmost care. My body is also one of those details. And while I am "in shape," it is important that I build my form to be as ideal as it can be as an additional accent to the picture being painted for her to observe.

Spiritually, I know that physique is not important. But, care and respect for the details is – which means if there is something that I can strive for until the day she finds me standing in the sand awaiting her arrival, then I will continue to strive for that ideal. But, as I strive for that ideal, the wear on my body brings a greater imbalance to my mind/body/soul. I have mentioned it enough in my journals, so the challenges it creates should be apparent. But, this is all part of the story that needs to be told.

So, as I've struggled to find consistent harmony when I close my eyes, I prayed before I went to bed this evening a long prayer about helping me find balance – a way to not miss the experiences that help to shape me so much. I also prayed to experience some type of interaction to bring me peace of mind in the weeks leading into the great days of the 15th and the 28th with Lindsey. I asked God to allow for experiences with Lindsey's soul – something to bring calm to my nerves due to the gravity of everything upcoming; something that could let my soul know she is there waiting for me. I did not ask for it to happen immediately – just over the coming weeks.

The Written (cont'd)

And even then, I acknowledged that if my request represented a step backwards on my journey in holding faith in God, then I did not want to take any steps backwards. I essentially said, "If it doesn't hurt anything and can only help me out, then I hoped He would allow for an opportunity for my soul to commune with hers." It was because of this prayer and the event I am about to share, that I believe the tornado earlier in the evening was a grand wake-up call. This was a moment God grabbed my attention and said "Get Ready" because He would show me a grand gesture hours later as I meditated after waking up this morning.

    I found myself standing before a great angel. Lindsey's soul was standing next to me. We were both groggy in a spiritual sense – awakening to the moment. As we stood there, I looked at Lindsey. We did not speak – we just looked at each other and soaked it in. It was obvious we were both rationalizing the moment. Eventually I mustered up some words that were undoubtedly broken and out of context, but I just wanted to speak to her. I asked her if she wanted to go somewhere with me. She said she did. We walked. We talked. We shared a lot with each other. I could tell her soul and mine had found song. All I could wrap my mind around in the moment was that she really, truthfully liked me. It was not just a fairytale story – it was a reality.

    We eventually walked to a vehicle and sat down in the front seat. The vehicle's front seat was a bench – like in older model trucks. She slid into the middle seat and put her head on my shoulder. She found comfort in me. It made my heart

Rebirth II

melt. She placed her left leg over my right leg. My right hand rested on the inside of her right thigh – but not so much to be sexual in nature. My hand found a perfect placement in balance of Love and desire. I could have sat there for ages – and perhaps we did. Perhaps our souls are still sitting there as I write this. She was caught up in me as much as I was caught up in her.

Before we made it to the car we ran across several angels. My mind had not fully rationalized the world as the heavens and so I attributed some of the earlier angelic encounters as "family members." But angels are friends and family as well as creatures of divine character. It is an interesting divide in learning how to understand spiritual brethren. They continued to want to speak to me and meet Lindsey. When we reached the vehicle, I felt peace that it was just Lindsey's and my soul together. But as we drove – recklessly and at a high rate of speed I might add – I took notice of a police officer and knew we were about to get pulled over.

When we were pulled over I saw Lindsey try to figure out how to fasten her lap belt. She could not figure it out and did not want to get in trouble for not wearing a seatbelt. I was witnessing the same spiritual clumsiness I demonstrate when I am beginning to rationalize the experience is slightly different than the earthly experience. When we stopped, an officer summoned Lindsey to get out of the car and walk up a set of steps in the distance to the right side of the car to speak. I was nervous, but not for being "pulled over." Instead, I knew this was someone trying to alter Lindsey's spiritual course.

The Written (cont'd)

As she got out of the car, there was a group of angels standing on the street corner all shouting out to us. They were happy. They wanted to see Lindsey and me together. I identified them as my family. Several were sitting on the steps where she was walking to speak to the officer. Before Lindsey got out of the car, I made a joke about how my family seemed to be everywhere. I was somewhat embarrassed – but I would come to learn it was not of spiritual embarrassment.

So after Lindsey got out and walked up the steps, I decided to follow suit. As I reached her, there was one of the angelic elders sitting on the steps observing everything. I was trying to get everyone to leave us alone with the officer. It took me several attempts, but I finally was able to get the angel to get up and allow us some privacy. I felt bad about it, but there were too many circumstances that I felt the need to control. After telling the officer that Lindsey should be free to go, and that I would take care of her, he made a comment to me expressing his doubt.

As we chatted, someone ran up and took something from my back pocket. He knew the officer, and the officer allowed it to happen. I became angry. I asked why he did not chase after him. The officer seemed more content at throwing a wrench into the day with Lindsey and me. He eventually made some comment that made me reply something about wanting to punch the guy in the face that took that thing from me. It was wrong to have felt that type of frustration. I know this now. But in the moment, my spirit was on autopilot trying to protect Lindsey.

Rebirth II

The officer made some other comment about how I would not have the opportunity to do so, to which I responded, "You'll see. We will win." I assume I was talking about the longevity of Lindsey's and my possible relationship, but I honestly do not know what the words alluded to. The officer made some strange symbol with his hands and tried to fist bump me in a competitor-kind-of-acknowledgement way. But when we tried to fist bump our hands just went through each other's. I was puzzled. He laughed. After that, Lindsey and I began to return to the car, and then my alarm went off, causing my soul to return to my body.

Just as instantly as I opened my eyes, I recognized the error of my ways. I immediately prayed to God, and pleaded for forgiveness. As I talked through the situation and how great it felt to interact with Lindsey's spirit, I had twice as much guilt in trying to dismiss my "family" and preserve my time with Lindsey. As I came to realize in prayer, the autopilot feelings I was expressing toward my heavenly family was the result of pent-up emotions I had from my earthly family. For every relationship I tried to get involved in, somehow my mother and sister always attempted to wreck it, or at least express enough frustration at me that I would be shamed out of liking whoever was the focus of my heart at the time.

As a child, I learned to preserve my feelings by keeping relationships out of the eye of my family. This scenario was no different. While I did not have a full understanding of my surroundings and that my "family" was my heavenly family of angels – the ones who help me and guide me throughout my

The Written (cont'd)

time here on Earth, I went into self-preservation mode. To me, this means two things: 1) I must truly Love Lindsey. 2) My spirit is still weak.

I prayed to God and directed my prayers to the angels around me as well, asking – no pleading – for forgiveness. My earthly mind rationalized the scenario much more quickly than my spirit understood the scenario. And though I do not doubt this is the first of more experiences with Lindsey to come over the next couple of weeks heading into what I can only describe as the biggest portion of my journey so far, there were several important takeaways.

The first is that God again showed me His mercy and Love by allowing me to see and experience her spirit before the 15th. The second is that He exposed another weakness I must extinguish before the 28th. Finally – and I cannot emphasize this enough – I felt Loved by her. This was the first time I felt the Love of her spirit toward me. To date, it has been a one-way perspective with faith on the other side. This time, I experienced it in a way that I could understand her Love for me. And all of the angels – the family that I continued to see along the road as I drove Lindsey around – were all there to welcome her and me home together. Even by typing this, I again feel an overbearing sense of shame and guilt for how I acted. I pleaded for forgiveness immediately upon opening my eyes – and I know that God and the angels must see my heart as pure, but still scarred during my growth. I can only hope that I get the opportunity again to show Lindsey my

Rebirth II

true family – the family of angels that work so hard with my struggling soul.

March 10, 2014
Afternoon

During lunch, I prayed and meditated. And while I normally do not include my visions and spiritual experiences from meditations throughout the day in my journal – I feel this one, in particular, is important. My prayer began with me continuing to express my deepest apologies for my actions toward the angels – and by summation, to God. I continued to ask for forgiveness. This was the majority of my prayer before meditation. I ended my prayer with a thought that was running through my mind.

After the experience of the interaction with Lindsey, I began to wonder if the call to action that I have felt impressed upon my soul is not a call to action through the body as a vessel for the spirit, but rather through the spiritual experiences in heavens. Is it possible that for Lindsey's soul to be primed and ready for my Love, that I would have to interact with her spirit and show it all of the Love I have to give? I know in an earthly sense, that our souls find song in each other. But what if the romance of a soul is even more specific – more discreet in action? What if it is truly a spiritual interaction that occurs when our souls are not confined by our bodies? What if the experience with Lindsey a few hours prior was the start of romancing

The Written (cont'd)

her soul in a way that words and earthly actions are not required? Could this be what it means that my soul must learn to move without my body? Is this why I am figuratively standing in the sand while my spirit is running toward her? Could it mean that the very ability for me to be actionable involves my soul and hers interacting with great frequency each day and each night leading up to the 15th and the 28th?

These were the questions I began to pray for guidance from God in understanding. And while I left my questions open ended, I did ask that if this was part of the steps on the journey for Him to guide me – to groom me through the process. I expressed that I was ready to interact with her soul more frequently if indeed, that was the next step for me. But I also expressed a great thankfulness for the opportunities He has shown me with her so far and that I was not asking for more in a greedy fashion. This was an open-ended expression of my quest for guidance. After my prayer, I found guidance.

For a very brief period of time, I was able to find the right balance during meditation for my spirit to depart from my body. Almost instantly I was standing in a room with three different female spirits – one was Lindsey. They were all laughing and making jokes. One angel was with her boyfriend. As Lindsey was speaking about relationships, the couple slipped behind a vase that contained a large plant. They were all in an office – so imagine a planted tree in a pot that you would see in an office setting.

Almost immediately, the girl began to tease the guy sexually. And just as instantly, he climaxed. They stepped out

Rebirth II

from behind the tree. Lindsey rolled her eyes as if in disbelief, and also in recognition that they were happy together. She turned to her right and her eyes fell into mine. We just stared at each other. She saw me. She had bright red lipstick. The strength of the moment was so grand I lost harmony and returned to my body. All I could think of was getting back.

I began meditating again – focusing on my balance. Instantly, I was transported back to the office setting. I invited Lindsey and the other uncoupled girl to another floor in the building. Immediately I returned to my body. I was finding it extremely hard to balance my soul and body. I meditated again, quickly returning. This time, I was on a different floor in the building. As I stood there staring at a doorway bathed in darkness, Lindsey and the other girl appeared in the hallway. They had taken the elevator to this floor. For some reason I thought it was "down" when we were all "up" earlier. I also knew this to be the eighth floor.

I looked at Lindsey. This time, I was an observer. I do not think she could see my spirit. The girls were bubbly – excited at what they were to see. As if I was a guide to them, I willed them to look inside. Or perhaps, I felt their will to look inside. As they approached the door, a curtain was pulled back revealing an elaborate setup – like that of a stage show for a professional band in a quaint theatre environment. As the curtains were pulled back, there was a purple/mauve drape hanging from the ceiling with my name, "Jonathan" written upon it in gold script.

The Written (cont'd)

This is the first time I have ever seen my name in the heavens. Once before I heard my name called out from an angel. These are the only times I have felt identity in the heavens. I have to believe that if my identity is in fact my earthly name, then it stands to reason the mark I will leave on Earth after my time here is complete must stand the test of time tied to my first name. But in this moment, I just observed.

Underneath the drape the light was turned on, revealing a group of probably six or seven angels working on the setup. The girls just stared. I just stared. All I could comprehend was that we were on the eighth floor, looking at something being prepared for me – and being prepared in a way that Lindsey and her friend were able to witness. As I made eye contact with an angel in the room, I lost harmony and returned to my body. Immediately I began to pray to God in recognition of my awareness of the experience. I also realized that while I had prayed to interact with Lindsey's soul if that was part of the journey, He immediately cast me into that scenario. I could honestly tell that I saw a spiritual representation of how she was interacting with her peers at work in that exact moment.

By this point, I no longer questioned the validity of these types of experiences. To date, every experience that I have attempted to verify/prove as real has been 100% verifiable in the earthly world. So, now, I just take this in stride as my soul interacting with other souls on Earth. Each experience is new. Each experience is a building block. For me, this may be the first time I have interacted with someone in this particular

Rebirth II

manner – where I saw their earthly walk through the interaction with their soul. The two do not exactly correspond, but they do in an archetypal sense – which is the important aspect to be gleaned. The spirit and the body are not tantamount to each other in form and physique. Instead, they are tantamount to each other in archetypal existence – in spiritual flow.

My first reaction upon returning to my body was, "Wow. That was a lot harder than I thought it would be." Just being open and honest in my journal – this particular experience was extremely taxing on my ability to maintain harmony and also to find traction in the midst of the spiritual flow of active, daily spiritual routines. Now I imagine that in the early morning hours when people rest, traction is easier to come by since it is akin to awakening the spirit, which is still groggy in understanding. But throughout the earthly day, the ego takes control leaving the spirit to fend for itself. What I witnessed was the spiritual form of the egoic interactions on Earth. Tough. Tough to interact with, but I know this is another step in moving without the body. But my major takeaway from the entire event was that God helped me lead Lindsey (and her friend) to a room that had my name on it. Her soul had to identify my name – which would transcend as a spiritual seed into a thought in her earthly mind. The interaction was akin to gardening her thoughts. I guess that is the best way I can put it with my best efforts in expounding upon the situation with my limited understanding of All That Is. But this, at least, seems the most probable explanation. The big question I took away

The Written (cont'd)

from the situation was "Why eight?" What is floor eight metaphorical to in a spiritual sense?

After reflecting on the experiences in the heavens, and later through a conversation with Bryan, he immediately understood the meaning of "Floor Eight." There were no questions in his delivery – and even after his explanation, he felt led to tell me that his interpretation was at least one of the truths the vision held. Bryan explained that "Floor Eight" was metaphorical to the same thing as "turning the volume up to eleven." While he used analogies from martial arts and how in one form, there are twenty-four belts of which no one on Earth will ever attain belt twenty-four. He explained that "Floor Eight" represented an unobtainable level of achievement while on Earth. Number seven holds within it all of the connotations of God's fingerprints. It is His divine signature on everything He places in our lives. If the earthly understanding of the world is always in divisions of seven (as I have written about in Song of The Spheres), then "Floor Eight" represents the divine, enlightenment, ascended master, etc.....whatever name you wish to ascribe to it. This does not mean that I have obtained that category – far from it. But, for me to see a room of angels preparing a room for me with my specific name on it, located on "Floor Eight" essentially was a way to showcase to me what I should continue striving for. It is a destination that is metaphorically being prepared for me as I grow in spirit. Bryan called it a birthing room. For, when my days here on Earth end, and assuming I continue striving toward that ideal,

Rebirth II

the room on "Floor Eight" would be metaphorically where I would be birthed.

Now, as I write this, do not take the words of birthing room literally (or really any direct example I have given). For the experiences in the heavens are archetypal...metaphorical in context. And while it remains to be seen how literal they will eventually become, the delivery of the experiences are optimized and efficient means of communicating to the soul, without impeding the journey. They are guideposts. So, with that said, I also feel at peace with his interpretation. It speaks a truth upon my soul.

March 11, 2014

I had a very difficult time meditating and even sleeping last night. I obviously have had a whirlwind of thoughts running through my mind – but it is disappointing that I was not able to calm the storm of thoughts last night for a prolonged period of time. However, there was one moment that I can recount with some clarity. I, again, was allowed to find the company of Lindsey's soul in the early hours of this morning. We danced to music played by a pianist. At one point, the pianist began to play "Her Man" by Gary Allen. When she noticed the song, Lindsey stopped dancing and looked at me. It was as if she queued into the moment and achieved a state of lucidity and awareness of her surroundings. Prior to that, it was as if we were just two groggy souls dancing.

The Written (cont'd)

But it was at this moment when she looked at me and asked, "Is this 'Her Man?'" I said that it was. She looked at me confused. It was as if she was trying to rationalize everything going on. She fought with the idea for a moment that "Her Man" was being played while she tried to understand where she was standing. I am not sure of the significance of that particular song in her life, but at this point I have to believe that it holds an access point to special memories for her. As she looked at me, I continued to give her confidence that we were indeed dancing to "Her Man." I even hummed along to it. She leaned back in and rested her face on my right shoulder/chest. We continued dancing slowly to the music as the angels stood around us, watching us fall in Love.

March 12, 2014

The first experience is somewhat vague. I was standing in a house with an angel and another soul. There were suit jackets lining a wall – each made of a thick, luxurious fabric. Each jacket was different and had different patterns and colors. They were not vibrant – more subtle and subdued in design. But each jacket made a statement. While we were speaking with the angel, he disappeared but returned wearing a nice suit. He mentioned that it was important that he wear a suit/blazer/coat. Words were not stated clearly, as the conversation was archetypal in nature again. But it was my impression that he was saying that he needed to wear a coat,

Rebirth II

but not for purposes of climate. It was at that point that we talked about how I could not recall ever seeing him with a jacket on before. He laughed and showed us the wall of suits, coats and blazers. He talked about how we just were not around when he needed to wear them.

The second experience took me to a beachfront location. Most of it took place on a patio outside of the back of a white building/home. The patio had two tables surrounded by chairs. There was a dividing wall between the patio and the sandy beach beyond it, but a walkway leading out into the sand. Prior to walking outside on the patio, I had been in a deep discussion with a female angel. It felt very much like she was a motherly figure, and I a child. And while I just described the scenario in a way that evokes images of age, I would describe it more along the lines of she was my elder in heavenly knowledge and had been guiding me in a maternal way.

The discussion we were having involved the use of a "drone" to help me tell the story that is being played out in my earthly life with Lindsey. I would not say I was scolded, but it felt as if I had "gotten in trouble" over the prior days for invading other people's privacy with this "drone." Think of the drone like a toy, and I, like a child playing with a toy. However, I think the drone was more symbolic of my own ability to peer just a touch into the future and help affect the landscape of the story playing out in my earthly life. And while I was being told to be careful in how I used the "drone," I knew the ability to use it properly was important. It seemed necessary to help shape the story that will one day be told on Earth of how

The Written (cont'd)

Lindsey and I interacted as I fell in Love in what would appear to be a moment of near-instant brevity. Think of the drone as a plane with a camera that gave me a lens into another soul's life and actions. The drone allowed me to understand life through their soul's lens of view.

We continued to talk a lot about the drone, but the angel also seemed busy talking to other angels that came and went. It was as if I was being babysat in a way...again, not to be mistaken in an earthly sense...but similar in concept. I spent what seemed like days in this house. On the evening Lindsey was to arrive, we sat outside on the patio. My motherly angel shared in conversation over drinks/dinner with two other angels at one of the tables. I sat at the other table by myself playing/learning about how the drone worked. While the angel knew I was up to something with the drone again, she let it slide as she was having dinner. For some reason, it seemed that there was another device I needed to make it work properly. Logically, I still do not understand how the devices tied together, but the "controlling device" looked like a sewing machine. It was large and sat on the table where I was sitting. I studied it, trying to understand the logic with it. Perhaps it was more metaphorical to the fabric of the aether....but it will require more meditation to understand what the purpose of the sewing machine was.

Eventually a friend of mine who knew how to fly the drone came over from the beach. I wanted to make sure I had backups to help me fly it when Lindsey arrived. This preparation occurred for a while. It was very important that I knew

Rebirth II

this was in preparation for her arrival and that she was not present in this particular circumstance with me in the heavens. I suppose the drone could also be metaphorical of her plane flight to Jacksonville I had planned for her and her family (unbeknownst to her), but again, I will need to pray for guidance and clarity on the matter.

I eventually lost harmony and returned to my body. It was clear I was working in a time period that preceded her arrival. Whether this meant her arrival in the heavens (as in she may be physically awake or not in the right balance of mind-body-soul, etc.) or arrival on the beach on the 28th, it is hard to say. Time is obviously relative to events, but in this situation, I did not know if I was traveling into a future point in time, or to a point relative to the present (give or take a little).

After returning to my body, I journaled the experience and tried to get back to the location from where I had returned. It took a while, but many hours later I was able to return to the heavens with a great state of awareness. I found myself in a room with a large group of angels/souls. There were probably twelve people or so in the room. Most all of the angels were female except for one black male. While I understood the group of women to be Lindsey's coworkers in context, I think "coworkers" should be interpreted as the family of angels helping Lindsey's soul grow...similar to the family of angels I am beginning to identify as my "family."

They liked me...they liked me a lot. They wanted to get to know me more. I cannot tell you what the purpose of us all being in the room was other than for us to get to know each

The Written (cont'd)

other. One girl came up to me and began talking. She was familiar. I had seen her before in the heavens when Lindsey was around. It is important to know I had never seen anyone who even remotely looks like this angel in my earthly life. She had blonde hair and was very pretty. Her name was Melanie. She chatted with me a lot – all of the while she continued to smile. Her friends also continued to smile. I could tell there was a loving happiness they were all embracing while I was there.

Eventually, I asked where Lindsey was. She told me she would "go check the calendar." When she walked away, a brunette girl came up to me and chatted. We talked about children. She wanted me to babysit her children sometime. I told her "of course I would." Perhaps I did not understand the context, because she said, "You would?" as if she was surprised I would be that open to it. Suddenly, I had the impression I was supposed to babysit them as soon as I left the building. I became confused. I knew I had my daughter this weekend and could not possibly babysit if it was going to take me away from introducing Lindsey to my daughter.

This was a point where there was a blending of my earthly and Heavenly walk. My mind fought the rationality. It was quite a battle of mind and spirit. Eventually the meeting came to an end, and I left the building. As I drove away, I felt guilty for not babysitting the children, even though I realized it was only Tuesday and I did not have Georgia until Friday. There was some high impetus to understand the intention of Thursday. I was not sure what it all meant, but on the surface it

Rebirth II

appeared I had time to babysit, so I turned around and went back to the building.

When I went in, there was another meeting forming with a subset of the people in there from before. The black man was on a stage talking to the other six or seven angels in the room. We all sat and listened to the man talk. He continued to make jokes and make personal remarks about me. They were good remarks – as if letting the women in the room know I had some quality that I did not quite understand yet. While I cannot explain how, I can say I managed to let the brunette girl know I wanted to babysit her children and that I just had to rationalize what was going on. I apologized. She was extremely happy I had returned.

This was almost like some version of mental telepathy as we sat there – but again, it is hard to explain. While we sat there, I recognized one of the angels/souls as "Lindsey's sister." Perhaps it was Lindsey's biological twin's soul. It seemed that way at least. I had never met her…at least I cannot recall having met her before. But in the moment, I knew who she was and knew it was important we talk. We chatted for a while. She seemed more guarded about me, but I could tell she liked me a lot as well (liked me as in liked me for Lindsey) – but, in a sisterly way. I could tell she was protective. She acted as if we would know each other forever – and I have to believe we will.

As we sat there, taking turns chatting with each other and listening to the black man, Lindsey came into the room late. She was in a costume or disguise. It is hard to tell what it

The Written (cont'd)

meant specifically other than she tried to mask herself from being seen. But, her eyes could not be masked. Despite a heavy layer of green face paint/makeup which made her look like she was at a Halloween costume party dressed as a witch, she was beautiful. She had a black hat pulled down over her head so as not to be recognized. I had the impression she had been out with her kids at some costume party.

I could tell she did not want to initially be recognized. She continued to cut her eyes my way, looking at me. We were sitting only a few feet apart, and I could tell she was nervous about the moment with me. Her eyes gave her away. I never let on I saw her, but I imagine I was probably staring – even though I tried to be discreet in looking at her. She eventually excused herself and went to clean off her makeup. She returned unmasked before me and sat down next to me. She was beautiful – as she always is. Her words were short and simple. All she could muster was a coy, "Hi." Again, her nerves were easily recognizable.

As we sat there for a bit, she eventually warmed up and began to talk to me more. I did not want to pressure her. I wanted her to find strength in me. Eventually we turned to face each other as we sat cross-legged on the floor. She looked at me, and one of the first things she said was, "I really want to go out of town." I smiled knowing the surprise plans I had made for her and her children. Her comment was intended for me to say, "Me too. Let's go." She wanted to go out of town together. Perhaps her soul knows what the angels have been

Rebirth II

helping me prepare for her – all to be revealed over the next few weeks in our earthly lives.

When she told me she wanted to go out of town I said, "So you aren't going anywhere over your children's spring break?" This was an important question for me to ask because the series of events to unfold for her hinges on her being in town to check the safety deposit box and going to Nordstrom before the flight out of town. It is a question I plan on asking her when I see her at the coffee shop on Saturday. She just shook her head "no" in response. In this moment, I felt a rush of relief and a newfound burst of confidence for the upcoming events. I also understood it to mean that she really wants to meet my daughter and see me this weekend.

While we chatted, I never told her that we would go out of town together. But, in the way she continued to speak, I could tell she wanted me to ask. I have to think that her "family" must know about it and have been helping set her expectations with me. There was one point in our conversation that I reached out with my left arm and touched the bottom of her right forearm in conversation. It was important I established touch. When our souls touched, it electrified my soul. It felt so real in an earthly sense. That moment kick started a "touchy" conversation where we each took turns subtly making sure we touched each other as we spoke. There was one time we tried to hold hands, my left hand and her right. But, as we held our hands together, our palms passed through each other's hand. We looked at each other strangely knowing

The Written (cont'd)

that what just happened was not natural in an earthly sense, but we just kept talking.

Eventually I lost harmony in the moment, but the whole evening was grand. It was an answer to a prayer I had earlier in the evening wherein I asked God, that if it did not affect anything negatively and could only help, to allow me to continue romancing her soul. I also prayed for longevity in the heavenly experience by asking him to help me maintain harmony for a longer period than I normally do. Additionally, I asked for a heightened sense of awareness. The touch of my hand to her forearm was an answer to that.

Traditionally, I do not pray for such experiences as I assume that each experience that is presented is the next step along my journey. But recently, I have come to realize that there is a likely possibility that the intentional romancing of souls and interactions with the angels and souls in heaven is how the experiences manifest in our earthly walk. It is one thing to understand that the earthly walk should be approached with the same eyes of the spirit as I have witnessed in the Heavenly experiences. But now, it seems of utmost importance to be called into action in the heavenly experiences…at least in what God allows to happen. A child would not be told to go fly an airplane, just as a spiritual child would not be charged with something outside of his spiritual capacity. But for this point in my journey, I think it is important to see the parallel of the heavens to my earthly walk.

The experience of sitting on the patio earlier in the evening makes me think that the experience parallels to the angels waiting to watch Lindsey and me as we stand on the beach on the 28th. It may be difficult to put into words, but a call to action in the spiritual world could be seen as akin to planting seeds, or planting thoughts spiritually that will manifest in the earthly walk. As a seed needs nurturing, it is the spirit's call to action to nurture that seed in the heavens…where eventually I have to believe that the divide will one day merge and become one between Heaven and Earth, for this is how Heaven already exists around us…but this is just conjecture as I continue to learn what has been prepared for me on each step of my journey.

March 13, 2014
Early Morning

Only a handful of times has Lucifer shown up in my experiences in the heavens. Each time it precedes a great gesture from God to me. It is always at a time when my faith in Him must be demonstrated. Each time, Lucifer attempts to introduce doubt. This experience was like the others. I found myself standing on a platform. Lucifer was on a platform across from me. There was a chasm between us indicating he could not touch me…that we were on different planes. As we faced each other, I observed that he was again wearing a suit, no tie, had round glasses (not rose colored this time), and his hair had lighter brown highlights in it and was curly. His hairstyle looked somewhat like Sammy Hagar's hairstyle.

The Written (cont'd)

Lucifer kept telling me that doubt was important and tried to convince me that I had doubt in God. I continued to tell him that I did not have any doubt about Lindsey or the manner in which God was bringing us together. I said that I did not need doubt in Lindsey texting me back anything other than "okay" tomorrow. This was in reference to the fact that I would be texting her about the plans for her meeting Georgia on Saturday. It is important to note that when Lucifer entered into the experience, I felt a cold wave overcome my body and felt a disturbing vibratory state that tried to introduce anxiety.

As we talked, he tossed a black canister underhanded across the chasm to me. I caught it. I held it in my left hand. I was heading to speak to God, who was on my right. Lucifer told me that if I do not have doubt, that God's going to know. He said that God would discover the doubt (represented by the canister) when I arrive at the next destination tomorrow (this was represented by an image of a hotel – no doubt in reference to the hotel that Lindsey will arrive at as I stand awaiting her arrival in the sands of Ponte Vedra Beach).

I told Lucifer, "No He won't. I will take the doubt (canister) and cast it away behind me." Lucifer rolled his eyes at me and said, "Whatever…He's gonna know." I repeated that He would not. I became disgusted at Lucifer's presence and called my soul to return to my body. When I opened my eyes, I shouted out, "Be gone Lucifer, and don't come back." At that point, I heard God smile at me. I am not sure how to say it any other way that "hearing Him smile." The spiritual context in how God delivers His message is distinctly different than

Rebirth II

any other form of earthly communication. But, when I heard Him smile, I immediately felt a warmth around my body letting me know Lucifer was gone and that God was holding me.

I prayed to God in the moments following and at the end of the prayer asked Him for continued interaction with my spiritual family. Perhaps I did not clarify what I meant well enough, or perhaps God had other plans for me because I spent the next several hours of earthly time (days in spiritual time) interacting with the souls of my immediate earthly family in the heavens. I spoke to nearly each and every one of my family member's souls. Bryan was, strangely, not there.

I saw my mom, dad, sister, Rory, Meredith, my grandparents, and many others. Meredith and I spoke a great deal. I received some type of message from her when we began talking. There was a strange container of flowers shipped in a clear, rectangular package to her from the guy she was with. She was extremely happy with the flowers. They were received on Valentine's Day. It seemed that we were discussing a past event that still lingered with Love in her mind. We joked about the temptation of a delivery guy to see if he could make the flowers and water leak from the package before it was delivered to her. During the conversation, we also discussed my absence from everyone. I told her that I had been absent for a specific reason on my spiritual walk. She thought I had been ignoring her, but I clarified it was not her – it was all of my family that I had removed myself from for a while.

After speaking with her, I journeyed to a countryside where I saw my grandparents on my dad's side. I observed

The Written (cont'd)

their house, their farm. The grass was lush and a verdant green. I also observed a giant rocking chair unlike any I had ever seen before. It was handcrafted by my granddad. He was making two more, but it was important that I see the one that he had finished.

We chatted about it for a while, and I listened as he talked about the care he took in getting the farm completed for my grandmother. He was proud and was doing everything in Love for her. He pointed out the fences which were made of white stone/alabaster. They had black interwoven Celtic-knot squares adorning the corners. The knots had a 3x3 grid of holes in them. It was elegant, but obvious that it was handmade.

Eventually I left to find my parents. When I found them, we chatted for a while. We spoke about my absence. We spoke about Lindsey a bit. I wanted to show them my grandparent's farm. My dad had seen it at some point, but they wanted to go. We eventually arrived where it was apparent that my granddad was now working on the next two rocking chairs. There was a tremendously large block of wood that He explained to me was how he got the great curve of wood for the rockers. He explained why and how that block of wood was required to be used to build the rocker. I can only describe the block of wood to be something smooth, like that of the front half of a wooden shoe block that helps leather shoes maintain their form when not in use. I want to emphasize that these rockers were huge. They were intended for someone who must be two to three times the size that we were in relativity. I could

Rebirth II

only guess they were intended for great angels – or my grandparent's eventual great angel forms.

Eventually my grandmother called us all into the home. It was simple and rustic. The home faced the west to watch the sunset. There was a porch that was also being built to hold the rocking chairs. Inside the house there was a square table where my grandmom set out places for each of us. There were three glasses and a bowl of food for each of us. I was fascinated by a darker looking drink in one of the glasses. I picked it up and tried it.

It was a cinnamon-apple tea. The tea was thick, but extremely good. I drank most of that drink first. It seemed like a delicacy. When I reached the bottom, I could see that the remaining liquid at the bottom had a lot of floating spices that comprised the drink. After I finished the drink, I ate, and I drank the other beverages. None was nearly as vivid as the cinnamon tea. It was a flavor I had never experienced in my earthly walk.

After dinner, my grandmom was talking to my parents as my granddad continued working on the rocking chairs some distance away. My grandmom made a comment to my dad about how they were finishing everything out on the farm completely debt free. She explained that my granddad asked her for two years to complete everything on the property for her. He needed two years because that was the date "his retirement matured." She mentioned it was the same day that the account they had created for their children and grandchildren also began distribution. I could not determine what

The Written (cont'd)

context she was talking about, but it seemed she was referring to the distribution of abundance (of something unstated). It was not money, though that would be the earthly interpretation. We spent a long time on the farm and eventually left. When we left, I felt as if I had experienced days in the heavens – perhaps longer. As I thought about it all, I lost harmony and returned to my body.

March 13, 2014
Afternoon

During my lunchtime prayer and meditation I sought God for continued forgiveness for what I could only describe as a blunder of epic proportions I made last night. As strong as I have been in my journey into the Promised Land and following the directions God has given me with Lindsey, I have kept nearly the entire experience to myself. I have not shared with my daughter that we would be meeting Lindsey this weekend. Nor have I even shared with Bryan anything about my circumstances with Lindsey. So last night when I was speaking with my daughter on the phone, she asked me directly, "Am I going to get to meet Lindsey this weekend?" The last couple of times my daughter was in town, she was supposed to meet Lindsey, but the plans did not work. In the end, I know that God had His timing prepared specifically for this upcoming Saturday and the way the events would play out. But, each weekend prior when Lindsey was to meet Georgia, I did not

Rebirth II

know what God's plan was. So, it was easy for both myself and Georgia to become excited about the two of them meeting.

Georgia senses how much Lindsey means to me. But without mentioning her in any conversation over the last month since I saw Georgia, I was hoping to keep her shielded from being hurt by not seeing Lindsey. This is where I went wrong. Because, if there has ever been anything I have sought clarity in, and found truth in from the mouth of God Himself, it was that He has foretold of the day Lindsey and I would meet so that she would receive the book I have written and kick start the chain of events that would unfold over the next two weeks.

But when Georgia asked me that particular question, I froze. I did not know what to say. The proper thing would have been to wield the word of God with confidence and say, "Yes. We are meeting her on Saturday" despite not having confirmed with her in an earthly sense. Spiritually, it had been confirmed. God had confirmed it multiple times. I should have had no thought to obstruct God's words from flowing through me. But, in that moment, my mind became an obstruction. I knew God was speaking through my daughter, testing my faith. Even with that, I paused. I said, "You'll have to wait and see."

She pressed onward. She told me how she hoped they would meet. I asked her why. She responded in such a spiritual way – explaining in her limited words what her soul was trying to express. I heard it. I heard her. I heard the voice of God tugging at her soul, helping her piece words together. I

The Written (cont'd)

began to open up with, "That is the plan," and "We are supposed to, but we will see." With each reply, I introduced doubt. Eventually, I stopped myself and just said, "You know what Georgia? Yes. Yes we will see Lindsey on Saturday. This has been the plan for a while, but I was trying to keep it a secret."

And while I eventually said the right response, I felt a weight of previously unknown proportions fall upon my soul. In all that God has provided for me and in the way He has helped me with such care along this portion of the journey, all I had to do was say, "Yes." But I stumbled. I fumbled and nearly lost the football. It was a moment that I recognized how I was nothing without God. The moment when I understood that He was fully in control. My soul knew it, but my mind tried to protect my daughter. But what was I protecting her from? I was actually protecting myself. And if I was protecting myself, what was I protecting myself from? The only answer is doubt in God's amazing power. He is everything. He provides everything.

I must have prayed for hours before bed last night, and this morning I awoke pleading for more forgiveness and mercy. I have been on such a straight and narrow path – so close to the destination – and in the final steps I tripped up. I knew it immediately in the conversation with Georgia. When I hung up the phone, I immediately turned to God asking for forgiveness. If anything, there was only one acceptable answer. That was "Yes." And by missing that step, I recognized that God could take everything that He had promised away from

Rebirth II

me in an instant. I did not know if He would…but I knew He could. This was not just a roller coaster I was riding. I could make missteps.

So at lunch today, I continued to seek forgiveness and ask for clarity. I had messaged Lindsey early in the morning making sure about times for Saturday. And while I knew she would take a while to respond, I also had peace in this being the plan all along. This was the day I would reach out to her. This would be the day I would send a ping of my spirit to hers and wait to hear a ping back. It was the metaphor of pings on a spiritual radar. As I prayed, I let God know I was not worried about not hearing from her – and truthfully I am not. I have no discomfort or anxiety over prompt replies from her anymore. This is all about the destination God has intended, and my eyes are straight ahead.

In prayer, I continued to ask God for opportunities to demonstrate my faith. I wanted Him to see that I was truly sorry and would wield His truth unquestionably. I had made the same prayer this morning, and last night. I asked Him to be gentle with my heart, but I acknowledged I had no right to ask Him to be gentle on anything. If anything, I know God saw my fear in His power, my desire for His mercy, and my humble servitude to His calling.

The events of the day began with me arriving at work and stopping to pick up a cup of coffee from a small eatery stand inside the office building in which I work. It is run by two beautiful souls. Every time we speak, I always question whether they are angels. I always hear God speaking through them.

The Written (cont'd)

And, in truth, they seem to know more about my spiritual life than I ever let on. They know events before they happen.

This morning Glenda asked me what I was doing this weekend. The manner in which she asked it, and the context around it made me know it was God speaking through her. This was my opportunity. This was my first chance to prove to God I had faith. I replied, "I am introducing the Love of my life to the other Love of my life – my daughter." She smiled. She told me "how great of a day it would be" and gave me confidence. When lunch arrived and I drove to the church soccer field that I usually go to eat, then pray and meditate, a car pulled into the parking lot with a flat tire. I knew this was God's calling, part two. I turned around and went back to see if I could help the man. After making sure he was taken care of, I continued on to the soccer field to eat my lunch.

After lunch, I prayed and spoke to God at length about all of my thoughts. In the end, I told God that all I knew to do was to continue on to the destination unfazed by my blunder. I wanted it to be clear though that I was at His mercy upon the outcome, and I knew I made a grand mistake the previous evening. But I did not want it to cause me to stagnate on my journey. I asked for His guidance in how I should carry on. That was the most important thing – asking His will. I also prayed for Him to help me understand His forgiveness and mercy in a way that I could recognize. I elaborated on how I had never been in this situation before – in any aspect – the good, the bad, the missteps, the recoveries. It was all new to

Rebirth II

me. So all I could do was seek His guidance and ask Him to show me how to continue forward.

When I meditated, my spirit was allowed to travel to the heavens. My soul began wrestling with a wolf. The wolf was about to bite me on the neck. It was so close to taking my life, but in a moment of brevity, the wolf quit moving. I realized I somehow had shot the wolf in the neck with a gun in my hand. There was no sound. There was no silencer. The wolf just rolled off of the top of me, and I could see the hole through its neck. After this, an angel spoke briefly to me, but the words were lost as I lost harmony with the moment and returned to my body.

I immediately let God know that I had understood His message. The wolf represented the fear and doubt that was preying on my soul. And while I had the ability to ward off the wolf with the weapon in my hand, I never fired it – which leaves the only explanation as God "firing the bullet" that rid me of the wolf. He helped me. As I sat in my car thinking about the experience, I felt a great weight lifted off of me. I knew that God had forgiven me. In the end, God helped me see that my fall/stumble was more like a clogged pipe than falling down with absolution. My mind/body is a pipe – a giant conduit for God's voice to be heard – and it was clogged. Last night, God helped me unclog the pipe in my delivery of His word. Knowing the incident was more like unclogging a pipe than self-destruction on the way to the destination, I found confidence to continue onward. But this was not the end of God's answers to my prayer.

The Written (cont'd)

On my drive back to the office, I saw in the not-too-far-off distance two people standing beneath one of the large blue food signs that precedes each exit on the interstate. While I drive the interstate often, I have never stopped to look at the sign as I know the area very well. In the few seconds from when I first saw the movement of the two people standing beneath the sign, they quickly turned and walked into the trees. As they turned, I saw their wings. These were angels sent by God with a message for me to see.

Directly between where the angels were standing, was the sign for Starbucks. Unlike every other sign I have ever seen, it was not aligned in a tiled fashion on the sign, starting at the top left. Instead, it was at the bottom of the sign, in the very center. Truthfully, I am going to have to go back to see if the sign really exists or if it was placed there by the angels for me in that moment. I cannot imagine it being that out of place on a commercial road sign. (I will update this entry when I do double-check the sign).

So why is Starbucks important? Well, in the text I sent Lindsey, and in the visions that God has shared with me about where we would meet, it was always in a Starbucks. This morning's text to her was confirming that we would meet at a Starbucks between her house and mine...not the one on the sign I just passed. That specific sign was not important. Instead, what was important was seeing two angels on either side of a Starbucks sign to let me know to maintain my course and keep my sights on the destination.

Rebirth II

So at this point after my prayer, God shared with me an experience in the heavens with the wolf. Then, He placed two angels before me with a sign indicating the destination. But, He was not finished. After I exited, about a block before my office building, there was a car that was broken down. It had just pulled over to the side of the road. The car was still slightly blocking traffic in the right hand turning lane though. I pulled into my office and immediately turned around to go help. I knew this was another test of my spirit.

I went back and parked near her car on a side street. I noticed two other cars with their hazard lights on as well. All of this had just taken place, so there was a lot of spiritual movement going on. I got out of my Jeep and headed to her car alongside another guy. Another man had just reached the girl's car prior to us. He began pushing the car up the hill toward the side road. Immediately, I and the other guy began pushing. It would take the three of us to get the Honda up the hill so that she could then allow it to coast down the side street and into an open parking space.

As we crested the hill, the car picked up its momentum to head down the hill. Each of the three of us headed back to our cars. As I got in my Jeep, one of the guys who seemed to know the girl, shouted out thanks. I turned to the man parked two cars behind me and just stuck my hand in the air as if to say, "Thank you, brother." He just did the same – mirroring back my motion. We all departed. As quickly as three people can swoop down and help someone, I witnessed this very pace in an undoubtedly spiritual event. That girl (whose car had only

The Written (cont'd)

broken down seconds prior) was held by God's hand through the calling of His vessels. It would take all three of us to muscle the car up the hill – a feat that would only become apparent as we were pushing it up the hill and feeling the weight of the car.

Perhaps the other two were angels. Perhaps the girl was an angel testing others on their walk. Perhaps it was just a spiritual collision of souls wanting to share Love and help. Words were not spoken. Action was all that was required. And, pace was important. It seemed important to get in, get it done, and get out – leaving only a simple gesture of spiritual recognition at the end to let each other know it was the work of God. Or perhaps each person was an angel sent to mirror back my spiritual and physical gestures, letting me know I took the correct spiritual action in the moment. I suppose that is the great thing about spirituality – the reasons, actions, and outcomes are always multi-level in construct. And it is unto each of us to learn to accept every possibility as a potential truth along the journey as we demonstrate our spiritual walk on Earth.

Update on 3/14/2014: On my drive into work this morning, I double-checked the placement of the Starbucks sign. It was indeed placed at the bottom middle of the blue food sign. I also observed it is located at mile marker 70 (which reduces to 7 – God's signature). After I observed it, I watched as two birds took flight from a treetop beside the sign and flew across my path. This was one last great sign from God. Two birds has become a recurring theme for myself and Bryan...from the dove and the hawk, to the two birds that got my attention when I was pleading to God for help on understanding which direction to take a few weeks ago

Rebirth II

with Lindsey, to the two birds that entered Bryan's house. This was undoubtedly one more great sign of His divine work.

March 14, 2014

Last night was an extremely busy night when it comes to experiences in the heavens. I believe this is partially because I have taken the last three days off from working out and have allowed my body time to find harmony again. I know I need to get back to working out for the 28th, but it was important I find clarity and balance with my jaunts to the heavens. But before I write about the events of the evening/morning, I wanted to write about a couple other things that happened from the time I awoke through my travel to work this morning. While I do not normally write about all of the ways that God communicates with me throughout the day, I think that in light of the event He has planned for me on Saturday, I should try to write everything I can.

So, when I awoke this morning, I immediately wrote down the last monumental experience and turned to God in prayer. I gave Him thanks and praises for all that He had continued to show me. I picked up my phone to check my email. There were seven messages. In earthly terms, this may seem like a coincidence – but I assure you this is another method of God echoing back His signature to me. After every action that I am called to do, there is always a way that God places His signature in recognition of the action. For me it comes in a va-

The Written (cont'd)

riety of ways. A lot has to do with the number seven. Sometimes it has to do with a pair of birds – as would happen later in the morning. But today, it was email. So after I checked my mail, I got ready for work and headed to my car.

Parked next to my Jeep was a car I had not seen before in our gated lot. It had a Florida tag. I did not think much of it at the time other than, "I can't wait until the 28th." But the important thing was that it caught my attention. It was parked directly on the right side of my Jeep. This is important, though I would not understand it in that particular moment.

On my drive in, I was lost in thought and prayer. When I drive on the interstate, I usually pick a lane and stay in it unless there is a really slow driver. Today the traffic was moving smoothly. As I was praying thanks for the signs God has placed around me, I noticed that the car I had been driving behind had a Florida plate as well. I live in Tennessee, so seeing Florida plates is not too uncommon, but the significance was about to be revealed to me in short order.

I instantly recognized that God was showing me that He was at my right side through the symbolism of the Florida plate I saw earlier in the parking lot (a divine symbol of the right hand of God). Florida represented the "Promised Land" of meeting Lindsey in Ponte Vedra Beach, FL on the 28th – all to be kick started by us meeting for coffee this upcoming Saturday. And now that there was a Florida plate in front of me, it was meant for me to understand that God was at my front – and I was just to continue following His path. As I prayed acknowledgement of seeing His fingerprint and following His

Rebirth II

lead, the car moved two lanes over to the right. I thought about it for a brief second, and decided that I should continue following "His lead."

I moved over two lanes to continue driving behind the Florida plates. I prayed out loud that I did not understand the metaphorical reason why I was following a Florida plate in my car, but if it was only to acknowledge that I was following His lead, then that was what I needed to do. After saying those words, the car exited off to the place I normally go to pray during lunch. I smiled. Just as suddenly, I recognized that there was now a car directly to my left with Florida plates – the third Florida tag. At first, I thought it was symbolic of the trinity – and perhaps it was. But as I said aloud to God that I saw the plates, the car slowed down and then proceeded to move behind me into the same lane I was in. The symbolism could not be more grand. With Florida being the metaphorical Promised Land that God has foretold to me on my journey, God was metaphorically parked at my right side, leading me, moving to my left, and then giving me a foundational push from behind. It was a counterclockwise motion that represented left-handed polarization – again a divine symbol. As I prayed aloud in recognition of seeing how all of the signs aligned – signs that would not have aligned as divinely if I had not "followed" the lead of the Florida plates in front of me and proceeded to move over two lanes to the right.

It was at this point that the blue food exit sign came into view where I witnessed the two angels standing along either side of the Starbucks sign yesterday. The sign was clearly

The Written (cont'd)

there, oddly placed in the middle at the bottom. At this point I recognized that God had brought my attention to something that had been there all along, and that it was not a sign placed there specifically for me yesterday. Though I still acknowledged God's divine architecture in having the angels draw my attention to the sign, He placed one more sign before me. As I passed the sign, two birds took flight from the top of a tree adjacent to the sign and crossed the interstate before me. The recurring symbol of two birds, sent to demonstrate recognition in what I did witness yesterday was indeed God's work.

From opening my eyes to the arrival at my office, I would have thought that would be the end of the signs from God to start my Friday, but He continued on. Yesterday, I asked God to continue testing my faith in Him and the date of the 15th. I wanted to prove to Him that I had complete faith. When I arrived at the coffee stand at the downstairs eatery, Glenda's husband David greeted me and we said our pleasantries. He asked me what I had planned for the weekend. I knew in that moment that God was testing me again. I looked at him and told him, "I'm introducing the two Loves of my life to each other on Saturday...my daughter and the girl I'm with." I struggled with phrasing Lindsey's identity because I normally do not give names during any conversation, but I did not quite know how to say, "The girl God has promised for me." So, instead, I said, "The girl I am with." David became excited and told me how important of a day it would be for my daughter and me. Again, I heard God's voice coming through David. I have always seen David and Glenda as angels – from

Rebirth II

the very first day I arrived in the building. This time was no different. After I paid for my coffee and headed to the elevator, I overheard him telling Glenda about all I was doing this weekend in a fatherly, bragging kind of way. It made me smile some more. Such a divine morning and I had not even arrived at my desk.

Shortly after arriving at my desk, I received a voicemail from Sara at the bank where I was led to open the safety deposit box for Lindsey. Yesterday I had left my contact information in a message to her and told her that she did not need to return my message – that I just wanted her to have my information for when Lindsey comes in. But this morning, she returned my call and emailed me to make sure she understood everything in the message. I emailed back just asking her to let me know once Lindsey had opened the safety deposit box so I could align the other plans. It was my hope that I could let Nordstrom's know with more finality which day to expect Lindsey to arrive. I was hoping they would have a room setup for her, but they needed more clarity for the actual day she would arrive. I suppose my request could be seen as just curiosity to make sure that I did not have to alter the dates for the hotel reservation and plane tickets, or prod Lindsey along to finish the book…and perhaps I may have to prod her along. I am not sure how that part will play out. But I do know that God has the end points in place. However, I do want to make sure I am not being too complacent and am prepared to act in whatever means necessary to help Lindsey if God calls me to action. But most importantly, the reason behind having Sara

The Written (cont'd)

email me when Lindsey arrives is to ensure that I can align Nordstrom's plans to have the dressing room prepared for her ahead of her arrival there. It is a nice polishing touch that adds an extra level of detail to the story. And while I know that many of the events that I have planned for Lindsey have not been disclosed in detail in my journal entries thus far, I still feel it is important to capture everything I can from this point forward.

Now onto the experiences in the heavens from the early morning hours before I prepared for work. The first experience in the heavens was unlike any I have had before. I recognized my soul as not having form. In fact, it felt that my soul was distributed across several objects – held together by my consciousness. The objects seemed like database servers for a company. I immediately realized I was like unto a thought at that particular moment. As I realized this, I began envisioning my soul as a body. As soon as I did, the setting transitioned to me standing in a formal meeting room with a long table. It was futuristic in design – like something out of a sci-fi movie. The room had glass walls around the back and sides. There was a wall and a doorway behind me. A small table was on my left. It was made out of wood. Everything else was made of blacks, grays, and whites – all with a sheen. There was a group of elders sitting around the table. One female was standing at the head of the table on my left side. There were probably around twelve people sitting at the table.

When I arrived, they turned to look at me. I began speaking about how the most important thing – and the reason I

Rebirth II

was there before them – was "for the soul." I wanted them to recognize I understood the importance of the soul. A man got up from his seat and walked toward me. I thought he was coming over to show me "a soul" – as in how they are housed without form in the heavens. But as he walked to me and began to talk, his words were broken. They seemed glitchy, like a computer malfunctioned or did not render his animations correctly. All I could think of were "glitches" but he could just as easily have been having a seizure...or I suppose I could have been losing harmony with my form in the moment and the "glitches" were my recognition of losing harmony. He had a large belly, but looked pregnant rather than fat. As I stood there trying to rationalize the "glitches" and trying to understand what he was attempting to tell me, I lost harmony with the moment and returned to my body.

After journaling the event, I found harmony again and returned to the heavens. Before me were large wooden tables laid out horizontally. Behind the tables was a wall with large pieces of paper hanging on it. It was setup like a registration desk at an earthly convention held at a hotel (or something similar). I stood in front of the table that was prepared for me. I looked up at the list hanging on the wall before me and began reading the words. It was a list of "to do items" prepared for me. Everything on the list seemed dimmed out except for one line item. The dimmed out (light gray) line items were illegible, but represented tasks that had been accomplished. The one bold printed item remaining said, "Waltz with her soul." The list was talking about Lindsey and referenced a prayer I

The Written (cont'd)

had earlier in the evening. As I read the line item, a large number seven lit up at the top of the sign acknowledging it was God's direct communication with me. The number seven was to catch my attention. As soon as that happened, I lost harmony and returned to my body.

I immediately journaled the moment and returned to the heavens. This was a much briefer moment in experience, but it held within it a powerful message. I stood before a black metal wireframe rack – like the kind of two-tiered rack that would hold newspapers or magazines. In the middle of the rack was an oval sign that had two lines on it. The top line was bold and large. It read, "Her Man." Beneath those words was a line that read "Jonathan & Lindsey." As soon as I read the oval sign, the rack twisted off and disappeared into the distance. I lost harmony and returned to my body.

The fourth experience in the heavens seemed to last forever, and was a test of spiritual strength. I found myself in the form of a child. I was approached by a group of other children that forced me to go to a run-down house with them. This was their house where they made sure I knew they made the rules and dictated how everything happened there. I was told of a "game" they played where they tried to kill each other – leaving only one remaining. They showed me how they used fishing twine and metal line to choke and decapitate each other. I was told that if I wanted to get out of the house, I would have to kill everyone.

I was not up for a game of killing anyone. They forced me through the dark house to a door. They opened up the door and pushed me through. I fell down into a pool without water. It had graffiti on it like you would see at a skate park. The only way out was to scale a near-impossible wall back up to the door that I was originally pushed through.

The pool was enclosed in a room with panels of square glass windows surrounding it. One large rectangular window was located beside the door for observers. Several other kids jumped into the room – all eager to kill. They held twine stretched across both of their hands, clearly to be used to choke and kill others. They asked if I was ready to kill. I immediately responded, "No. I am not doing this. This is stupid. I am not killing anyone."

I immediately scaled the wall and went out the door, chased by the kids. They all wanted to kill me first. I ran through the house and up a large stairwell that led to a large stained glass window at the top. The stairs were divided with a metal bannister in the middle. When I reached the top of the left side of the stairs, a couple of the kids were in hot pursuit but ran up the right side. The "leader" reached me first. I stood possibly three or four stairs from the top. He was on the other side of the bannister, eager to kill me. He began to lunge over the bannister at me. As he did (and when about half of his body was over the rail) I shoved him down. The force of my push sent him tumbling down the flight of stairs where he cracked his skull and was killed immediately upon impact.

My heart was heavy. I did not want to hurt anyone. All I wanted to do was not let them touch me. The kids looked on in disbelief. They circled his body in shock that their "leader"

The Written (cont'd)

could – and indeed did – die. They had been led by this kid for some time, and it seemed that he was invincible to them. They all feared me at that point. No one would touch me. I immediately tried to find a phone and call 911 for help, though I knew he was already dead.

When I picked up each of the phones, they all were without dial tone. I picked up the body and carried it to the passenger side of an old beat up white car. It was a two door 1980's style sports car in very poor shape. I placed the body in the passenger seat and drove him to a house that resembled my old home when I was married. I left him in the yard under a tree. I immediately called 911 for help. They asked for my address, which at first I blended two earthly addresses together – my last house and my present address. I quickly realized what I had done and corrected it to the address of my old house. As soon as I did, I became concerned I would be held accountable for the death.

I went out to the car where I could see my bloody handprints on the car door where I had carried him and then shut the door. I tried to wipe it off with a cloth. I wiped down any other place that could identify me with blood on my hands. I then went back in and tried to figure out how to dispose of the towel. But as soon as I got inside, I heard the police sirens. I looked outside and there were several cars responding to my call. I walked outside and showed them where he was laying. I decided the best course of action was to be completely transparent and true. After all, there was nothing I could have done to prevent the situation.

Rebirth II

A taller, black female came up to question me about the events. She had curly hair that was cut extremely short – especially along the sides. I explained about being kidnapped by the kids and that they were trying to kill me. The detective-lady seemed to understand in entirety. She did not arrest me and told me I would not get in trouble for what I did. She made it clear that I did what I was supposed to do and could not be held accountable for the horrible outcome that happened.

After our conversation, I was taken with her to the house where I had been kidnapped. It was in disarray. The kids there now had no leader, and no order. The children looked at me in disbelief again. This time they could not believe that nothing was going to happen to me for killing their leader. The detective took them all under her wing. I did not have the perception they were being arrested – or even getting in trouble for their actions. Instead, it seemed like the lady had found new souls that needed help and she was going to take them under her wing to give them guidance and help. This vision was incredibly detailed and long in both spiritual and earthly time. As it came to a close, I was returned to my body.

One last experience happened before I would rise for the morning. This was an experience that mirrored another recent heavenly experience. I was standing amidst clouds. I was standing upon a bronze colored hand. I was in the palm and there were fingers fanning out around me. There were more fingers than one hand has, so perhaps it was two hands held

The Written (cont'd)

open like a book. Whether it was one had or two hands, I knew that I was standing in "God's hand."

As soon as I understood where I was in the heavens, I was returned to my body where I prayed thanks to God for His Love and mercy. It was then that I checked my phone and saw seven emails – a divine stamp of his acknowledgement to my acknowledgement of the experience – especially the last one. I knew that God was telling me to relax and allow myself to be held – that He had everything under control. I know this was partly in relation to the meeting with Lindsey on this upcoming Saturday even though I still had not received a response back from my text to her last night.

Truthfully, the reason behind not texting me back yet doesn't matter to me. How can it? I know that whatever her scenario is, God is taking care of it. He is working it all out. All I have to do is be held and go to action when called. Absence of texts should more be observed as a longing to hear the spiritual pinging from her soul. I know she is there. I know God has us held in His hands. Whatever she is going through – if anything – is outside of my lens of perspective. God has this process held together in His hands, for He can act in any way required for the outcome. He created everything and can alter anything as He sees fit. This is faith. Circumstances are tossed out the window with faith, because truthfully – anything and everything is possible. All you have to do is believe.

At lunch, I went to my usual place to eat and pray. As I sat in my Jeep between the three churches that sit adjacent to each other, I felt called to not just pray at the soccer field, but

Rebirth II

to go into the smallest of the three churches and pray. After I ate, I headed over to the church. I had never been in it before. I had never even been in their parking lot for it was separated from the soccer field parking lot.

I made my way to the church and went inside the darkened sanctuary where I spent a long time praying and meditating. I knew God was present. I felt the tug in the middle of my forehead/bridge of my nose...the slight pressure that exists frequently when I hear God's voice directly, or when my soul departs for the heavens. This time, I never heard a reply, though my soul was not bound by my body. I was formless in the great expanse, praying to God for guidance over my next steps leading into Saturday. I prayed that He would help me know if I was to do anything, or if I was to just let it all be and let Him take care of getting Lindsey to the meeting.

I never had a response, but I felt more at peace about it all. The prayer was not limited to that topic only. I of course prayed about other areas of my life, but this is the most upfront and pressing part of my walk that I want to ensure I document. After I felt my prayer time was complete, I returned to my Jeep and returned to work. On the drive back, I received a call from a number I did not recognize. When I answered, it took a minute, then a voice came across that said, "Oh. I have the wrong number."

I glanced down at the phone number. It summed to seven. I was not surprised. This was God again revealing Himself to me in confirmation of prayer. I do not go seeking out num-

The Written (cont'd)

bers throughout my daily activity, but I have learned how God chooses to communicate with me in a type of handshake fashion. Did the call originate from someone trying to call someone else? Possibly. Was it an angel on the other end? Possibly. The circumstances do not matter – only the face value of what is being communicated. In this case, it was seven. Then I noticed something I had never stopped to take notice before. I only noticed it when I was adding the numbers. The area code summed to twelve, which reduce sums to three. The next three numbers before the dash summed to fourteen, which reduces to five. The last four numbers summed to eight, which is the same in reduction. This means the sequence was 3-5-8. These are numbers in sequence from the Fibonacci sequence. Again, a divine signature. If I wanted to verify that the number seven was not just randomly raining down around me today, this was an additional divine stamp that said, "Hey – check out the architecture of this one buddy." But it did not stop there.

This number was three-fold-confirmed in divinity. For if you were to take the area code – which was displayed in brackets – and place it alone, it sums to twelve, which reduces to three. It is also important in symbolism to see that the final seven numbers sum to twenty-two. This is representative of completing the progression of the twenty-two archetypes – the ones I have written about in Book VIII – Secrets. The last four archetypes of the sequence of twenty-two are located in the same archetypal place I stand upon in my journey. They are (in order): Faith, Hope, and Love. The final archetype is divinity/the arc.

Rebirth II

These archetypes are numerically even represented on the days Lindsey and I are to unite at the beach. I only saw this in retrospect, but it exists nonetheless. Even during my prayer at the church earlier, I prayed acknowledgement in understanding the last steps in the spiritual archetypal progression (nineteen, twenty, twenty-one, & twenty-two). This one phone call, which many would dismiss as a randomly misdialed number, held within it a grand message. The message said, "Look at me. I am Seven. But wait, there's more. I am the Trinity (3) + 22. I represent the Father, the Son, the Holy Ghost, and you represent the summation of the three steps of 7 – the seven archetypes of the mind, the seven of the body, and the seven of the spirit. Unity with Lindsey is representative of the final 22nd archetype. But wait – if you look even harder, you will see that these numbers fall in line with the Fibonacci sequence. The first three numbers in the progression are the foundation – the Father, the Son, the Holy Ghost – and the next three steps are the extrapolation of All That Is into creation – which is You."

While I know that is a lot to take in over one number – this is how a heightened sense of the world around you extrapolates God's message and His answers to prayers. Often it comes directly in a real voice of God; God appearing before you; an angelic encounter; something almost paranormal in nature; but all day long, every day, God is raining down this wisdom to those able to see – tailored to each person in a way that each will understand.

The Written (cont'd)

This is not science, this is divine. This is the divide. This is why it was important to note it heading into Saturday. Each day has become increasingly more important to document in order to add clarity to how He speaks. I have omitted a ton of daily moments like these, for I see most as an ongoing conversation with God – not a specific experience in and of itself. But this one was an experience and a conversation combined, so I included it.

When I returned to work, I was greeted by Glenda at the eatery. She called me over to chat. She asked if I was having dinner with my daughter and my _____. I put a blank, because Glenda was looking for me to fill in the definition of what this girl was to me. I guess I should have expected that after I typed out my thoughts about not having a specific way to handle the definition of what Lindsey is to me yet. So, as Glenda paused for me to fill in the blank, I said "Lindsey." She said, "Now, is Lindsey your little girl?" I said, "No. My daughter is named Georgia." Glenda smiled and responded, "Awww. That is such a sweet name. So Lindsey is your fiancée-to-be." She smiled. I smiled back and said, "Yes. Yes she is."

It was as if God just spoke directly to me through Glenda and told me, "Hey Jonathan – here is what Lindsey is to you. She is your fiancée-to-be." The funny thing about the whole conversation is that I have not once told Glenda or David anything about my situation. Only in the recent weeks has Glenda started talking about how I have changed and how I have a glow about me. She talks very spiritually, and I generally re-

Rebirth II

spond with answers to questions like "who is she?" with answers like "a very special person God has placed in my life." She knew nothing more than one sentence about my personal life. But, somehow, Glenda knew my whole situation without a word spoken. I know she is an angel and a very close, kindred soul. I responded only with, "I assume whenever God intends it to be." This is about all I have ever said to Glenda, but she knows. She is all knowing like the angels I see in the heavens. She already knows everything about me.

So, today when I came in from lunch and she gave me those answers, it was just more continued confirmation from God of the events. Then Glenda went one step further. She asked, "So are you having dinner with her and your daughter?" I told her that we were just having coffee. She smiled. Then she looked sternly at me. I have never seen Glenda look at me in any other way than happy and loving. This was different. These were eyes like the eyes of an austere angel ensuring that I received the gravity of the message involved.

Glenda said to me with this austere gaze, "She better not be a bitch about it. If she is, you let me know and I will take care of it for you. You are special, and if she is half the person you are, it will be perfect that she was there." Then Glenda continued on, "I think it will all be perfect. You don't have to worry. Everything will go just fine. It will all work out." I just smiled and agreed – thanking her for her words of support. I knew these were the words of God coming through Glenda.

She even went on to say to me that I was family to her, and that she would take it personally if it all did not work out

The Written (cont'd)

perfectly for me. Honestly, as I type this, I am speechless. I cannot believe how amazing of a conversation that was. And for whomever may read this journal entry at some point in the future, it is critical to understand that I buy a coffee and a muffin most mornings from David and Glenda and just exchange pleasantries. That is as simple as our earthly interactions have been. But Glenda and David's spirit shine through the dark, illuminating the downstairs entranceway to the building each morning. Our souls know each other – and likely have for quite some time. I am sure they are angels among my spiritual family, watching over me.

March 15, 2014

This morning's experience would be difficult for me to explain as "in the heavens" – though it most definitely took place there. The experience lasted days if not weeks. But, the scenario was in the Jacksonville, Florida or St. Augustine, Florida area. The theme was centered upon my new directive to move to Florida. In the experience, I had a temporary apartment on the waterfront that was in a four or five story building made of alabaster. It seemed to be on a bay/or inlet because the water was calm and there were no beaches in sight. Perhaps it was on a lake or river delta. But, there was a marina outside the back of it. The location was very nice.

I had been traveling back and forth from Nashville to get my stuff moved down to my new apartment. It was located in

Rebirth II

another part of town, but also on the same waterfront. To reach the apartment/house/residence, there was a long L-shaped boardwalk. The house was on the water adjoining a series of other houses. It was sort of like a large warehouse that had been converted into living units. But it was important to understand it was all resting upon the water – not the land. This was a specific symbol.

On the last day of my move, I was bringing my daughter down, and my father wanted to help me move. We placed large bags in the back of a trunk and made the drive from Nashville to Florida. My dad was excited to help and have me near. He was really surprised at how nice the residence was, and was intrigued by the location. It was not as if the residence was necessarily expensive or lavish. My impression was on the spiritual representation of the residence. It was a place that had been prepared for me upon my journey. The whole experience involved the duration of completing the move and the daily living activities while in the temporary apartment. I have to assume that the temporary living residence was metaphorical to Nashville and the new residence "on the water" and that was "prepared for me" was metaphorical to the next stop on my spiritual journey.

The next experience included no visuals, only symbols, words, and voices. I was only in a liquid-like spiritual form – not in the form of a human soul. During this time, the word "cheese" and the date of the 15th were paired together. Shortly after, I was pointed to the book of Judges – then the number twenty-two. Since the experience occurred the morning head-

The Written (cont'd)

ing into the date I am to meet Lindsey for the first time outside of the church environment, I have to think this was directly pertaining to her. I tried to seek out verses or chapters fifteen and twenty-two in the book of Judges to decipher His message to me. I tried every pairing I could.

His message ended up being the story of Samson and Delilah – which is interesting because earlier in the day, I had been thinking a lot about that story for no apparent reason. Also, if anyone were to ask me where that story is located in the Bible, I would not have had the slightest idea. I never was aware it was in The Book of Judges. Nor, do I believe I have ever read that particular book in its entirety. Anyway – it was some food for thought going into the day.

In reflection of the events of the day – and after not meeting up with Lindsey today – I still am unsure how any of the experience and His message parallels. I have wondered if the experience is possibly intended to be some type of parallel to me and Samson, and Lindsey & Delilah…but, honestly – I have no idea how it is would even be applicable.

March 16, 2014

After a spiritually exhausting day of wielding my faith in meeting Lindsey on the 15th – even in sharing the entire story with my daughter and how God had told me that today would be the day, I found myself entirely at a loss in how I seemingly misunderstood God's words. My daughter and I talked about

Rebirth II

it for a long time. She was my angel – my saving grace in sanity for the evening. I felt spiritually naked and broken before her.

At the end of the day's conversations, we arrived at the action possibly being the most important thing we could have done. For, God had never said we would necessarily meet that day. That was my interpretation of His call to action for me. His answer was in direct response to what day I needed to try to give Lindsey the book I finished and set the plan in action. So, as I went to bed, I prayed for clarity. As I found balance in my mind, body and soul, I found myself in the heavens with "the girl" angel that is like a mother figure to me.

We were standing in a train yard with several passenger trains around us. She was asking me in what ways God communicates with me – what types of symbols. The only answer I felt like I could explain with absolute spiritual clarity was in the symbols of trains. So, as she asked me the question, I responded simply, "Trains."

She replied, "Good. How so?" I did not even have time to muster an answer before she asked me to board a train. We stepped onboard a train to Chicago. When we arrived, we stepped off the train. She asked me how many people I thought we spiritually helped on the journey. I said three – for it seemed like I could only see three people around us. She told me I was wrong and that I helped seven. She also said I saved a child's life by being on the train we boarded instead of another train.

The Written (cont'd)

We continued boarding trains and repeating the exercise. The angel kept asking me how many people I was helping each time. I would always say how many people or how many seats I saw available. I was always wrong. It was always much more. There was always another train right behind us too. We boarded three or four trains, each having the same questions drilled into me. Eventually, the experience ended, and I returned to my body. My immediate takeaway was that I should do as God instructs without clouding the directive with why I think God is saying what to do.

On my way back from dropping Georgia off, I had a moment of spiritual breakdown with God over the frustration of not having met Lindsey yesterday. The 15th was a day I had long been told was the day I was to give her my book and set things in action. I was even told to not communicate with her for weeks prior – which was almost impossible to do. I again found myself shouting out in my car trying to understand what I was doing – or if I was doing something wrong. If anything at this point, I have only seen potential in outcomes and not tangible results with Lindsey. Each time God has spoken to me has been so powerful, but the earthly divide left me feeling like I could potentially just be losing my mind.

I shouted out for clarity as I drove home. I explained to God that it was just Him and me – that I had no one else to turn to – and should have no need to turn to anyone else. I apologized for the yelling, and explained I was not mad at Him. I was just spiritually redlining on my walk of faith. How can a person walk by faith when every result I led myself to

Rebirth II

believe was about to happen went without resolve? If my walk was truly just God and me, He was going to have to witness me breaking down because I could not maintain anymore spiritual strength in that moment.

It was like a child crying in front of his father. I was embarrassed, heartbroken, and losing my faith. As all of this was happening, I prayed out loud for peace. Suddenly the car in front of me began to brake and grabbed my attention. The car had a Florida license plate. Of course it would. God had been filling my life with this symbol for the last week. I took notice and asked God if He was telling me to just focus on Florida with Lindsey. I asked for clarity on whether I should just go lob the trip up at her and say, "Hey – its all paid for. Come on down." Or, perhaps I was to continue on with the path I now was unsure of – the path of giving Lindsey the book to kick start the events.

I pondered whether it was possible that the man in rose-colored glasses was interfering and if God decided to allow it to happen to see how I handled the situation. If that was the case, then I was most certainly supposed to continue undeterred by this apparent breakdown from reality this weekend. As I was talking about all of this and taking notice of the Florida plates, I began to acknowledge that I was listening if, in fact, I was not truly losing my mind. I thought I was about to just break down completely.

It was at this point that my phone lit up with several messages. Again, this is another typical form of communication. One message was from Bryan saying he was busy and could

The Written (cont'd)

not talk. This was definitely an acknowledgment from God about my earlier point about it just being Him and me. I knew that Bryan was not who I needed to confide in. He never tells me he does not have time for me – and it had been weeks since we had talked, so it was definitely a divine intervention. I acknowledged my understanding to God, and sent a quick reply to Bryan to which he promptly responded, "Always." Another sign. He had never said anything like that in texts, nor have I. What is important is that everything about my book is centered around my signature "Always, Jonathan." That signature recurs throughout the book. It is even on the back cover. So this was another sign that God was telling me the book was still correct.

The second message was a tweet from Lindsey. She posted about the sermon from church that morning and mentioned how unlovable and a wreck she was. It was in that moment that I knew God was showing me why we did not meet up yesterday. But she also posted a picture – and this is when everything again, fell into view. The picture was from the handout at church. It was discussing how "less is more" and how she was personally fasting from relationships.

On the handout, there were talking points about "fasting" and spending forty days in the desert. She also wrote down a verse: Psalm 63:1. Every bit of this paralleled to how God let Lindsey fall into my view during my forty day sabbatical. This was again, divine intervention. In my last text to Lindsey yesterday, I told her I was trying to deliver her something that God wanted me to give her on the 15th (this was my last ditch

Rebirth II

effort to show God I did not fear wielding his name, and that it was my intention to act as called upon). I even said I would drop it off somewhere or with someone to give to her, but it was met with no reply.

    Obviously I was limited to basically almost zero communication because anything more than one or two texts would be "too much" – so I danced around her one reply delicately. I could tell she was hurting. This is how she acted the first time we were going to meet – on her invite, not mine. In an earthly sense, most people would accept this as someone who is not interested…and I was beginning to border on this being a possibility, and that I was quite possibly just losing my mind. But, I tried to just be held by God. This was the root of the conversation. So, in seeing her picture, I realized that I was supposed to give her the book still. For the chapter that she is introduced in my book is called "40 Days" and is about my sabbatical and spiritual fasting.

    I got back to the house and spent the next three to four hours praying about what I was to do. I did not know if I was called into action, or if I was told to push pause….or possibly to even hit eject. Anyway, as I prayed, I suddenly was filled with a sense of spiritual action. I sprang to my feet and went to Wal-Mart to pick up supplies. I was to craft a box with special care and drop it off at her office for her tomorrow. Everything about the place I am in on my journey pertains to "standing in the sand" and "leaving my body behind" while I allow my spirit to do the talking. So, I figured it was not necessary for my earthly body to be present to get her to Florida – only my

The Written (cont'd)

spirit – which is encased in the words of the book I wrote. This was what I felt God was telling me, but I cannot say I had complete confidence. But, if nothing else, it gave me something to do that evening and to hope for in the morning. So I spent the next several hours putting together a self-folding box that was first wrapped in tissue paper, then with lace fabric on the outside.

It was elegant – perfect. It was handmade and communicated everything I could not say in words. I had never done anything like that before. I had never even used a glue gun prior to buying one that night. As I crafted the box, my phone lit up with another tweet from Lindsey. She mentioned a song that she has been listening to on repeat – and that was "her song for the day." It was a David Nail song called "Brand New Day." I had added it to my playlist in days prior, but had not listened to it because the first few seconds of the song sounded boring. But, now that I saw that Lindsey found something special in the song, I was now curious as to why I even added it to my playlist. I decided to fire it up and see what it was she was listening to – what her soul found a voice in.

The song could not have summed up my spiritual action and the church service's results with her soul any better. The song was about finally being out of the rebound and starting "a brand new day tomorrow." I acknowledged God's grand architecture and design. It was basically a starting line. This is when an earlier experience in the heavens began to make sense. That experience was the one where the angels helped Lindsey board the train with me standing there – though it

Rebirth II

took a lot of effort. I was told to "help" but did not see how my actions actually helped her board the train. This was what happened on Saturday metaphorically. Now it was up to me to waltz with her soul – a directive given to me a few visions prior.

March 17, 2014

While these two experiences were very abbreviated, they were in response to my prayer before bed. I prayed, asking for guidance in making a decision on the job offer and with Lindsey. In the experience I was driving around a road with subdivisions in Florida. It was a wooded road. The entrance to the subdivision I was supposed to observe was called "The Lakes." I lost harmony shortly after trying to see any more detail aside from those words.

In the second experience, I was running around the office I work at now. My cubicle was larger and was built for a large man – likely twice my height. I ran around the office like a child for some reason unknown to me. When I walked near the larger cube I felt pulled into a kneeling position. It was as if my spirit was called to kneel. I heard a voice say something about "stepping down." Then my name was shouted out with authority from an angel – but this time, it was my first and last name. This was the first time I have ever heard my last name from an angel's lips. This caused me to return to my body instantly.

The Written (cont'd)

When I opened my eyes I immediately journaled the experiences, and prayed for guidance. It would seem that they pertained to me stepping down from my current job, though it is possible that it meant to not take action with Lindsey. I prayed a lot about this for clarity. I asked God that if I was misinterpreting it, to let me know. I acknowledged I had a clouded lens since I am obviously head-over-heels for Lindsey, and that I would stand down if that was his directive. But if it was for work – which is what I thought it was – then I would take that action as required.

After much prayer, and asking God to let me know if I was to deliver the package at Starbucks to Lindsey today, I felt confident that my actions were filled with every good intention possible. I asked for guidance. I asked for clarity if I was wrong, but this time I received nothing that would alter my plans. So today, I dropped off the box and coffee for Lindsey's office. It was important that I felt the need to have it there by 10:30 – though I could not tell you why. It was the same feeling that I had the last time I felt the chocolate needed to be delivered by 11:00 only to find out the office closed at 11:30 that day. So, I can only imagine it is all well in action and delivery.

March 18, 2014

This morning was filled with numerous trips to the heavens. Every trip echoed themes of interacting with the souls of

Rebirth II

other people I know on Earth as well as with the angels. The first experience involved a discussion with a great angel. The angel spoke with me about how leaving my job would now be of utmost importance because I would now be involved in speaking engagements that will arise from the themes in the book I have written.

I can only imagine that by putting the book out "into the open" when I gave it to Lindsey, that I will now be tasked with supporting the words I have written. This was not a bad thing by any means. In fact, I took it as a good thing on my journey. But it also meant that the future would be built upon this decision – which was overall, spiritually led. I could not tell if the explanation of "speaking engagements" was akin to preaching, or if it was just to answer questions that may arise from the book – but it all seemed to pertain specifically to the book.

The second experience involved the job opportunity with Wilson. We had a great conversation and came to an agreement on the terms of the contract. It was at this point that we had some sort of business dinner. At the end, the bill was $357 dollars. I was asked to pay – of which I immediately panicked because all of my money is currently tied up in this trip to Florida with Lindsey. I decided it was a test.

As Wilson watched whether I would choose to pay, he began to ask questions – as in, "What is wrong?" and "Is everything okay?" and "You have the money, right?" I decided that since God had placed this contract as well as Lindsey into my life, they both should be treated with the same faith. I chose to go ahead and pay the extra $357 dollars on faith that

The Written (cont'd)

God would provide a means to pay for everything with Lindsey. After all, everything thus far had been a test of finances as well as the introduction of Love – so I decided it must be intended to ensure my ego was not interfering.

There was another experience where I talked with Jason's spirit. We talked about old friends – Brittany and Jenny specifically. We talked about how good souls they were and how they really needed to find someone to Love. I mentioned Jonathan C. as well – saying he had a good soul. But Jason did not seem to agree. Perhaps it was not Jason's spirit, but instead it was an angel that my mind was justifying as Jason. Either way the conversation centered around catching up on life and old friends.

The final experience was with Lindsey. We talked for an extremely long time. She looked completely in shock over the words she had read. This was no doubt her soul's pureness reacting to everything she began to read from my book yesterday. She was holding the book in her arms. She was definitely taken aback and nervous about the implications. But, the nerves were good nerves – as in, "Can this be real?" types of nerves.

She started telling me how she remembered the conversation when we first met, and then proceeded to tell me certain things that I had said to her – jokes that I had made that lingered in her mind. We laughed about it. I could not believe some of the words she was telling me because I sounded so goofy, but I suppose that is what was memorable about it. That is why she remembered it. I was also in shock she re-

Rebirth II

membered it so well. I hoped she had remembered that day, but I did not have any confidence that the words we spoke held gravity. As I tried to remember the words I said to her, I tried to repeat them back to make sure I said the joke correctly. I struggled though. We were clearly communicating spiritually, without words. But, when I tried to bring those words back to Earth with me, the effort to put the words in earthly context was tough, causing me to lose harmony and return to my body. But the conversation was grand. As we talked, she began warming up to me and I could feel her Love beginning to radiate a little more with each passing moment.

March 18, 2014

As I prayed and meditated after lunch, I had one more brief experience in the heavens. My prayer was about finding clarity in the finality of my job. I heard God's call, but was hoping to understand how I needed to transition smoothly. I also prayed that my actions with giving my book to Lindsey were just. I felt spiritually confident they were, but I felt that I would probably be left in a gap where I would not know for a while if I took the correct spiritual action. I felt that I did, but obviously this is the single biggest thing that has happened to me in a spiritual sense – so I have some fragility to the outcome.

My experience in the heavens was without form in vision, but I was present in spirit. I knew I was in the presence of oth-

The Written (cont'd)

er angels as well, though I could not see them. Suddenly, I heard a male voice – God's voice – that echoed throughout the heavens. He said, "Go home." I immediately returned to my body.

My first thought was in the literal – "Should I go to my apartment? Is something wrong?" But I immediately stomped that thought out. I knew it was of spiritual nature, so it only took a few seconds to find spiritual recognition in the words. It was God telling me to "Go. Fall in Love with Lindsey." He was answering my question as to how I would know if I took the correct spiritual action with delivering the book to her. At first blush, most people would wonder how I arrived at "going home" meant "falling in Love with Lindsey" but that is part of the story in my book. The Promised Land is the destination of Love in another – the place that God led the tribes standing in the desert in Deuteronomy. This was the place they were to grow and prosper – all provided by God's hand.

I also had made another analogy to "home" in my book – this one written well before my understanding of the spiritual journey being tantamount to the journey through the first five books of the Bible. The analogy I wrote about in my book about Love is, "If falling in Love is the leap, knowing you are in Love is pulling the parachute and just the glide home." I also recently felt inspired to write a maxim that I have not placed on Twitter or anywhere else yet, but it also used the destination of home as a metaphor to Love. The maxim goes, "Home is where the soul finds its counterpoint in another; it is not a specific location or place to be. We all long to be home."

Rebirth II

So, to sum up this experience – in response to my prayer, God told me, "Go. You have my blessing of Love with Lindsey."

March 19, 2014

In this experience I met both my mother and my brother. While my mind wrestled with this encounter actually being a meeting with the spirit of my earthly mother in the heavens, I think it is best to describe it as meeting my spiritual mother. I do not have a brother on Earth, so meeting my "brother" in the heavens definitely seemed to hold a greater significance to a spiritual family member rather than the earthly sense.

After meeting these two, I met my brother's father. I assume this description is important because it did not seem as if the mother and the father were in a relationship. The father and the brother were odd. They made fun of the way I looked. It did not bother me. But as they poked fun at me, I could not help but realize how goofy they looked. However, I did not let them know of my thoughts.

The two of them lived on a campground with tents strung up near an RV. They mentioned something about names where I laughed and called them "hanks." There was an emphasis on the "a" in the word hanks and the plurality of the word. I eventually found my mother again. She was shameful of them. She did not introduce my brother's father as my father, so I was left wondering if I was half of that guy's child.

The Written (cont'd)

Eventually we went to a store for clothes. While we were at the store, the two "hanks" appeared again. They wanted to fight me, but I would not. They were angry over something. It seemed they were jealous over my mother's attention toward me. The conversation turned to a strange conversation about clothes. They ended up making fun of what I wore, but I could tell their words were just protection of their own negative feelings of themselves. Somewhere around this moment I lost harmony and returned to my body.

My second experience involved a discussion with a blonde, male angel. He talked with me for quite a while about my past and the potential futures for me. He took a lot of time to tell me about the company I currently consult with desiring to hire me. I cannot really recall much more than this.

My third experience was as if I was allowed to experience an alternate timeline, such as a "what if" scenario. One of the brunette spirits I see frequently in the heavens was involved. I found myself knocking on the door of her home. She let me in. She was surprised to see me, but I could tell she liked me a lot. She has appeared many times to me while I was being tested with Lindsey. I was always careful to not show this brunette any emotion that would tug at her heartstrings. But this time, it was as if standing in her house was an alternate potential for what could have been if I had not been so driven about Lindsey.

While I stood in her living room with her (the walls were all white), I asked her what would have happened if I had shown her attention. She was hurt – I could tell. But, she walked up to me and said that she would show me. She began to kiss me and we began to make our way down the hallway to her bedroom as we were still kissing each other. She took off her shirt and I knew we were about to have sex. This is when my mental boundary came up because I knew I should not experience this portion of the alternate timeline. I immediately pulled myself back to my body because I knew I would not carry on any further with her, even though I instigated the meeting through my own curiosity.

March 20, 2014

Today I received three written and signed job offers on the exact same day. I had been praying for guidance on my next steps, and God had told me He would provide. I had faith, and in so, I saw His will multiplied around me. Deuteronomy 28:7 was a verse given to me by Wilson when we met to review his offer. This was confirmation of the plans I have on the 28th with Lindsey. That particular verse ends with a reference to the number seven.

I said a prayer before going to sleep last night after the conversation with Bryan yesterday. The prayer had to do with whether everyone is a projection of one's own self. It was akin to asking if everyone exists as one. Bryan kept repeating "spoiler alert" in our conversation which made me begin to piece together the concept of everyone as one. "Spoiler alert" is something that Lindsey said to me in the very first conversa-

The Written (cont'd)

tion we had. No one else around me has used that term, but Bryan felt inclined to use it repeatedly in our conversation. Seeing this little nuance brought forth the manifestation of my prayer on Earth. It is a concept as old as time, but cannot be understood until you can actually see the spirit in another through spiritual eyes.

Today at lunch, Bryan called with a projection of seeing his reflection reaching through a mirror and wrestling with it. I disambiguated it with the prayer from the night before and explanation of Love being the definition of two becoming one – which means that everyone and everything should be seen as one, bound by a universal Love. Love in another is the definition of the hand reaching through the mirror. Conversations continued throughout the day and evening. He sent tons of texts my way. The seventh text from him indicated that the angels disambiguated the numbers fifteen and twenty-two from an experience I had a few days ago. He was told that the numbers were pointers to The Book of Thomas (a Gnostic text). As it turns out, verse seventy-seven is pretty special too. The book of Thomas is the key to the Bible. It is the answer to all of the questions that cause contradictions. If the Bible is a cypher of sorts, the Book of Thomas is the Codex. The numbers fifteen and twenty-two came up in conversation because Bryan started using Samson as an example in conversation. I told him about my experience and how I was led to research the book of Judges from the earlier experience. We realized that each of those pointers were keys to our conversation, which eventually led him to Thomas.

Rebirth II

This evening I prayed asking God to take a piece of me and give it to Jason and help him find Him. I also prayed to take a piece of me and give it to Lindsey and help her find strength. I also offered my ultimate sacrifice to show Him I acknowledged His will – which was to demonstrate that He could take my life and help Lindsey find happiness – even if it was not with me – though I long for His mercy for our union. In all of these descriptions, when I say "piece of me" or "take my life," I mean "my essence." If we each have a finite amount of essence to give to everyone we can to help them find their way home, I wanted to express that I understood the concept and wanted to start subtracting quantifiable portions from my being in order to help others find happiness. All of this occurred on the first day of spring on a blue sky, cloudless day.

March 21, 2014

Today I will honor my vow to God and step down from my current MSI position even though that means walking away from the job security that once meant everything to me. I could not risk misinterpretation of His will. I know He has plans for me and I have faith that all I have to do is follow.

During meditation at lunch, I travelled to the heavens and found myself in a church. Off to the side was a group of angels in the choir loft. Following an angel before me, I walked by the podium where I reached out with my right hand to touch the

The Written (cont'd)

edge. I somehow managed to slice my thumb and it began to bleed, which jolted me back to my earthly body.

March 22, 2014

I found myself standing in a location called "Rome." I do not know if I was in Rome, Italy or Rome, Georgia – but my first impression was Rome, Georgia. However, in retrospect, I think "Rome" was actually intended to be the archetype for "advanced civilization." The city was slowly being flooded. There was one angelic couple who was looking for houses to purchase. I journeyed around with them in areas where the water had not reached. There were street names given to me along the way. They were important because they represented more symbolically than the street name itself. One street began with the letter N, though I do not remember the word. The other street was "Falling Down Street."

During the time spent with the angelic couple, Lindsey was with me. Eventually, Lindsey and I were put in a simple rowboat that could hold somewhere between four and six people. I rowed her through the water. I knew the water we were in was covering a partially submerged "New Rome" though it was not as deep as the water ahead of me. As we continued to row, I left "New Rome" and rowed into the part of the water that covered "Old Rome" – which was much deeper and more ominous.

Rebirth II

While we were over one of the deepest parts, Lindsey wanted to get out and walk to the shore. For some reason, she thought we were in shallow water. She did not understand the heavens, nor the water we were in. The body of water we were in was very dangerous and I knew that no one should attempt to even swim in it. When she stepped to the edge of the boat, I began shouting at her not to step off the boat. She plunged into the depths at a rate quicker than I can begin to describe. I immediately jumped in, knowing I was placing myself at risk. I could swim faster than she was falling. It was as if she was being sucked into the depths of eternal nothingness.

As I swam, I saw the submerged city/world that the water was covering. I swam approximately fifty feet before I managed to get underneath her and tried to hold her up. As I pushed upward, I could not do anything more than balance her in the water. I was quickly running out of oxygen due to the depth and the amount of effort I was taking.

Suddenly, an angel dove in and swam down to help. He was joined by another male angel. They told me to go to the surface to get air. I swam up while they tried to pull her up. When I reached the surface, I was floundering, but was managing to stay afloat. The pull under the water was strong, but I was stronger and could fight it to stay afloat. There was one more angel on the shore that said we would take turns diving in and helping out.

In a very short conversation, I asked what was happening to her. He said that she sank because of "something that happened before the flood." He jumped in to help the other two

The Written (cont'd)

angels. I reached the shore to pull myself out. We rotated jumping in to help pull her up. In the fury of the moment, I lost harmony, and returned to my body. I immediately prayed to God asking Him to help save her, and that I wanted to get back to save her.

March 22, 2014
Continued

I suppose I might as well make a note of this most unpleasant night. I knew this day was coming for sometime. God had foretold of me seeing Lindsey with another man tonight – I even was told who it would be from God. I continued to dismiss God's words in hopes that it was just fear and doubt creeping in. I am not even sure I journaled the experiences because I tried to keep myself in check with all of the journal entries pertaining to her. Isn't that a conundrum though? I would rather fight fear and doubt than have God tell me something bad was going to occur for me to witness.

Well, anyway, I have to assume there was a purpose to the evening. Tonight was the wedding reception for Jason – my used-to-be best friend during my egoic times. I did not want to go because I knew what I would witness, but I knew that I was supposed to go. I could not understand why I was going to have to witness it, but it was to happen.

Sure enough, Lindsey arrived late and met the guy I knew she would be with (Chris). It is extremely important to note

Rebirth II

that I have zero knowledge from outside sources on this, only what has been shared with me by God. She was wearing the same dress. The room was exactly the same. I first saw her in the same location that was imparted to me. It was like living a nightmare. She saw me when she entered and waved. She was extremely nervous. After all, I knew she had read my book and that my soul was naked before her. And now, she was in the same room as I with another person. She looked at me about every few seconds. I did the same, though. It was interesting to watch it all play out.

Earlier, before she arrived, an acquaintance named Chris was in the room standing by himself. Almost as a personal test, I went up to say, "Hi". I had not seen him in forever and everyone was so welcoming of my presence, I assumed that it would be a good moment of "Good to see you's" and "How've you been?" Except – I knew that I would know very quickly if he was with Lindsey (as God had shared with me).

When we hung out during my egoic days, Chris and I got along very well. We hung out a lot. But this time would be different. I walked up to say, "Hi," and his closest friends walled off in front of me. I played dumb. I said hello to everyone around him, catching up on the past. No one wanted to talk to me. I knew that he was with Lindsey and that he had found out about my book. I eventually shook Chris' hand. He did not even say, "Hey". He looked elsewhere and brushed me off. It might have been the coldest display I have experienced. I walked away knowing what God had foretold was true.

The Written (cont'd)

Later on she would arrive, and I would watch as he literally clung to her – making sure she was holding his arm the whole time. Honestly, she looked like she wanted everyone to know she was with him. So, of course I was devastated. I was not quite sure of the purpose – and honestly I am still not. Eventually she and Chris made their way near to where I was standing, reminiscing with old friends. He clearly did not want to leave her, but wanted to go get a drink. He left her in the company of an extremely large guy (that is one of his best friends) to watch over her. It was sort of comical. Lindsey wanted him to leave for a minute so we could talk, but Chris wanted her to go with him.

I took that as my queue, so I walked over and said, "Hey," to her and gave her a hug. We made quick small talk where she told me the book was "very good" and "very well written." It was not exactly the response I wanted to hear, but then again, it was not the scenario I thought we would talk about it. So I played dumb about knowing she had finished it. I said, "Oh you finished it?" She said she did. I asked if she had been to the bank yet for the safety-deposit box. She said she had not, but her girlfriends all wanted to go with her to check it. She said they keep urging her to go check it. I told her, "Just so you know, it is time sensitive." I did not want to reveal that there was a whole series of flights and plans booked ahead of her for her and her children, but she needed to know she needed to be actionable.

She looked surprised. "What do you mean?" she asked. I told her that she just needed to make sure she checked it

Rebirth II

Monday or Tuesday at the latest. She seemed confused. I told her to just "trust me." She smiled and said okay. With that I told her I would let her get back to her conversation, then I walked away. I said my goodbyes to some of my old friends and left the reception. It was all I could do to make it to my car. It was even tougher to drive home.

When I arrived home, I thought I was going to have a mental breakdown. So, I screamed. I prayed. I called Bryan. I unloaded everything on him that he did not know about...which was essentially everything with Lindsey. I struggled with everything I was witnessing. Even as much as I believe in everything God has foretold about her and me seeing each other on the 28th at the beach, I cannot help but feel broken and confused. Why would He send me down this path only to have it become destroyed?

I wrestled with the thought. The only conclusion I have arrived at tonight is that seeing her was necessary to get her to the bank so that she would not procrastinate. It also seems that the journey is not just about me and God, but rather me asking for Him to send in a battalion of angels in my time of need. I have struggled with this thought because I do not want Chris to get hurt, but at the same time, it would seem that the verses and everything He has been communicating to me recently indicate that people can be manipulated by either good or bad forces.

So I prayed. I asked God to spare Chris as a soul, but to send in His angels to annihilate Lucifer's forces. The only logic I have is that if God has foretold of a destination, and contin-

The Written (cont'd)

ues to support that directive, then the only thing that could be in the way is an opposing force. And, if there is an opposing force, then this must be a time that I have to ask for help. It is the only thing that makes sense, though it is with a heavy heart that I am even thinking about this. Perhaps this is where I have to acknowledge there is a real spiritual war, and it is not just a myth or a legend of each person's personal journey. Perhaps it is a greater force attempting to intervene during a person's walk. I of course prayed for guidance and understanding. But, I have to believe there is a destination that God wants me to reach, so I will continue on, asking Him to clear a path because I cannot do it on my own.

March 23, 2014

After I struggled to find harmony or even sleep during the night, I finally felt my body become charged in the early morning hours by the moon. This generally happens between the 2:00 a.m. to 4:00 a.m. timeframe. This is when I can feel my body begin to pulse to the energy of the moon. Tonight, when it happened, I shut my eyes and I immediately began a free fall into a tunnel. The experience was complete with rumble and a tremendous amount of energy. I arrived at a place that reminded me of Niagara Falls. There were a lot of people in boats above the falls, careful to not go near the edge. I did, however, witness some of the boats being mis-piloted and fall to the depths of the falls.

Rebirth II

When the experience began, I found myself standing on a dock. I was given a canoe by someone I did not know. The body of water was actually a green sludge. This was the same green sludge that was on Lindsey's face in a recent vision. I recognized it as the same, though when I saw her with the green on her face then, I did not know where the source originated. I just assumed she was wearing a mask.

So as I stepped into the canoe, it became submerged in the green sludge to the point that the edge of the boat became level with the surface of the sludge. A little bit of the sludge fell into the boat as it rocked beneath my weight. For some reason, I understood the sludge to be dangerous – as in I needed to stay in my canoe and not get out or let it touch me.

The person who gave me the canoe instructed me to journey out into the lake. I began rowing. There were extremely large boats everywhere with people on board. They could not see me as I navigated. I was rocked to and fro by the wakes of other boats and also from the larger boats inadvertently bumping me. At one point I saw a child with orange goggles drowning in the sludge as his father watched while remaining calm. As the kid was drowning, he looked at me in disbelief thinking I was "walking on water." In retrospect, I do not know if the canoe was figurative or literal. I assumed literal in the experience because it felt real, but I suppose it could have represented my spiritual vessel keeping me above the water as I crossed it.

As I reached the shore, my soul transformed to what I can only describe as a six-sided spinning shape that had a hole in it

The Written (cont'd)

with groove marks. If there is an earthly equivalent, I would say it was like a nut that goes onto a bolt – six sided with groove marks for the polarized threading of the nut. However, the shape was spinning at a rate too fast to fully understand the shape. I was very aware of the embodiment change – something that I had not experienced before.

    I was extremely confused as to why I was this shape, but as I began to ask why – I heard a voice of calm tell me that I was an embodiment of a "bad thought." Apparently, the bad thought that had arisen in my mind had to be exterminated. I was chased as I found a tunnel, similar to the one I entered the location. I journeyed into and out of objects. It was as if I shrank down atomically, then exploded into a full form upon exit. I knew it was a demonstration of how the spirit of God flows through all things, but I had never experienced it before.

    I left the Falls and arrived in an area of snow-covered mountains. I thought of the locations like the alpines. The chase continued for what seemed like forever. As it progressed, I was shared an understanding of what all I embodied as a thought. It was very confusing and likely too difficult to put into words. I eventually saw another "bad thought" become annihilated. It was after this that I learned that bad thoughts have to coexist with good thoughts for understanding to occur. I assume this was metaphorical to the stressful thoughts I have been having about whether Lindsey and I will really happen or not. I have been frustrated in my own inability to understand God's voice – so frustrated that I have been angry and

Rebirth II

mad. Apparently though, this is part of learning... and God showed me this by sharing with me this particular experience.

March 24, 2014

Today may be the most significant day I have ever experienced during my journey. While I had several experiences in the heavens, I was unable to bring them back with me. But, as I began my day, there was an air of peace and calm. It felt as if everything around me was in perfect balance. Last night, Bryan and I had a conversation where he felt very inclined to tell me about a new way of worship he was practicing. He was beginning each day in silence to allow God the opportunity to speak to him, rather than just pray and ask for a response. While I am sure on the outside, this may appear to be where "voices in the head" would be the popularly categorized explanation of this, please understand that there is a distinction between hearing voices and understanding how to listen for the voice of God.

Bryan explained to me several of the things imparted to him over the last several days. He was concerned I would think he was losing his mind, but I fully understood and accepted the idea that a conversation can be had with God internally versus externally. After all, prayers can be said in the mind. We also discussed how this offsets the potential for communication with God becoming ritual versus fluid, be-

The Written (cont'd)

cause this allows an open opportunity for communication in addition to the communication that is had throughout the day.

So, after reflecting on our conversation, I decided that I would attempt the same thing today. During lunch, I drove to my special place among the soccer fields near the three churches in Brentwood, Tennessee. I ate my lunch in silence. Afterwards, I prayed aloud to God explaining what I was going to try to attempt to do through silence. I reclined my seat in my Jeep and closed my eyes. As soon as I shut my eyes I thought the following sentence in my mind, "So, God. I assume this is how this is supposed to happen. I am just supposed to think about how I want to communicate with You and You will speak. So this is me listening for Your voice."

As instantly as I had completed the last word of that sentence in my thoughts, my phone rang. My first thought was that this must be the bank letting me know Lindsey finally arrived for the items I left for her in the safety deposit box. I smiled as I reached for my phone. Sure enough, it was an 855 number that could be the bank calling. I answered and only heard the tail end of a recorded message. The only thing that was heard when I clicked answer on my phone was, "664. Thank you."

It was obviously the tail end of a recorded message, but here is where it gets good. 664 reduces to seven (6+6+4 = 16, which 1 + 6 = 7) – the continued way that God communicates with me. As I say this, it does not mean that God communicates that way with everyone, or maybe even anyone else – but I know this is the way I have learned to listen for His voice. So

Rebirth II

as I sat there in disbelief, I processed the conversation that had just occurred. I said, "So this is me listening for Your voice." And God replied with a means he knew I would understand – the number seven.

Perhaps it held a dual meaning letting me know that at 12:08 p.m. Lindsey might have checked the safety deposit box as well – but, the overriding message was God's reply to my voice inside. This was the moment that marked seeing the inside in the same way as I see the outside – the final dimensional understanding of seeing the spiritual and earthly worlds as one. In spiritual texts, it is always said that one must learn to see both the heavens and the Earth as one and the inside the same as the outside. Today was the day of seeing the outside internally.

The day had already begun with this type of communication occurring to me multiple times, but this was the first time that it occurred in conversation with Him. Usually it is understanding when to take action by listening for His voice. But this time was different. As I sat there, I was overcome with emotion, but I pressed onward.

I shut my eyes and began to have fluent conversation in my mind with Him. As I spoke, I began to receive answers – but answers unlike anything I would have expected. I began to see internalized images imparted to me through this "wormhole" (as Bryan described it). I found myself being told to drive some form of spherical vehicle. It was a sphere that was part of three spheres spinning around themselves. I was told to just drive and not to open my eyes – just to listen for His voice.

The Written (cont'd)

In this moment, I did as I was asked and as I drove the vehicle down the road, I saw two birds and a carwash and came to a stop. In my mind, I heard, "Two birds on the carwash. Good." My mind was split in an earthly/spiritual duality. I could process what was going on in my mind, but was having a spiritual conversation inside. This is by far the hardest thing I have ever tried to explain in writing – but at this point I can only imagine a nonbeliever would think I am mad, and a believer would hold hope that what I am writing is correct. For me, this is truth and the unmistakably divine architecture to life.

As I sat there thinking about the two birds and the carwash, I recognized I understood the two birds, but had no idea what the purpose of the carwash was in the vision. As I thought about it, I heard a voice, "Follow me." Immediately, I began to journey down this "wormhole" and images started to fill my mind. I was only allowed to see certain parts of the location. The rest was intentionally shielded from view.

We walked into a room. I could not tell you who was leading me, only that I was being led. I was walked into a section of seats of which the seat on my left hand side (which would be the right hand side of the section) was brought directly into my view. It was clearly the "right hand side" chair because the design of the chair demonstrated an arching armrest on its right hand side and a flat side to its left, which was adjoining to something else, though it was shielded from view.

As I began to observe the intricacies of the chair, I heard, "This is your [insert word for seat/chair/place of rest]." I do

Rebirth II

not know exactly what the last word was because it held a connotation I had not heard before. All I knew was that I was told that it was my [seat]. As I observed the chair, I noticed that it was made of a plush grayish-lavender fabric. In the middle of the back of the seat were three letters all in upper-case script. The letters were T-A-J.

I thought about the letters. My mind raced back to being imparted the word "Teja" a year or so ago (that is my spelling – all I truly know is that it was pronounced TAY-YAH). I wondered if I did not understand how the word was spelled. Then I began to wonder if it was my spiritual name – though I had recently been called by my earthly name in the heavens. As I continued to observe this split spiritual/earthly duality of my mind, I began to think about the archetypes of the letters. I immediately recognized the importance of the letters. The first letter represented divinity. The second letter represented the strength of God. The last letter indicated right hand of God. These are the three most important archetypes that underlie the base of Hebrew, and I began to realize that I must be being shared a word that I did not know yet.

Eventually I pulled myself back into my earthly mind, though I felt like I was in a blissful world for quite a while after opening my eyes. I decided to google the word. Instantly, I realized that it was the beginning to the word Taj Mahal – the religious building in India. Still, I had no idea what it meant. I looked up the word and discovered that the origin of the word was Sanskrit. This should come as no surprise to me anymore. I continually am imparted Sanskrit words though I have never

The Written (cont'd)

read anything about the language itself. I have only come to understand that its basis is the same as the Hebrew archetypes. So, as I read the meaning of the word, I was overcome with such a moment that the heavens stood still around me. The word means "crown."

As my journey has progressed, I have continually asked God to groom me as a king (whether I am ever to reach that level or not). Receiving a crown in the Bible is not the same as popular culture would lead a person to believe. It is more of a recognition of God's recognition in your walk and that He is in you. Essentially, today I found the Kingdom within and was told by God that I was a King. There are no words that can do this justice. There is nothing I can write that can express the gravity of this moment. Honestly, I have no ability to demonstrate anything other than the conversation I had in words, for I have been shown that I am a King of a Kingdom not of this Earth. And with that, I have to assume the word that was imparted to me for the seat meant "throne" or some variation thereof. I can only surmise that when I was shown how the seat joined to something to its left, it would indicate something similar to the name of YHWH, which means "the right hand of revelation of the nail of revelation." I have a hard time even putting this into words because of how the implications could be misconstrued – or possibly there is nothing to misconstrue. This is what happened to me, and it is the grandest moment of my spiritual journey.

Second Revelation

There is a moment when a person's faith is tested beyond its bounds. There is a time when all seems lost until a precise moment of Divine intervention occurs and leaves the soul utterly spellbound. I think the only way I can describe this Second Revelation is to compare it to the story of Abraham and Isaac. There is a time in the Torah that God calls Abraham – the father of every religion to this generation of mankind – to take an unbelievable leap of faith in demonstration of His Love for God.

In that call from God, Abraham is asked to build an altar and make a sacrifice upon a mountaintop. That sacrifice would be to take his only son born unto his wife Sarah and sacrifice his life in demonstration of his Love and obedience. Though Abraham did not want to follow God's will, he knew he had no choice. As he tied Isaac down upon the altar and raised the blade above His head, the Lord called out from the heavens and said, "Abraham. Do not lay a hand on the boy. Do not do anything to him. Now I know that you fear God, because you have not withheld from me your son, your only son." With those words, the Lord sent a ram to be sacrificed in Isaac's place.

Rebirth II

While my experience is nowhere near a moment of life and death, it is the only comparison that can be made when the sacrifice that you have been tasked to make before God involves the most vulnerable part of your being. For Abraham, it was the Love of his son. For the time period it occurred, the demonstration of the sacrifice of a soul's Love had to be expressed in the most animalistic means. For before Abraham, there was no other whom God had shown more favor during mankind's time.

The record of Abraham and Isaac is written about in the twenty-second chapter of Genesis. And as it will eventually be revealed through the study of the Books of Nine as One, the twenty-second archetype – the twenty-second letter of the Hebrew alphabet – represents a decision, a choice. The choice that is made is a test of faith and a demonstration of the completion of the first part of the journey. For after this test, faith can be seen as Divine in His eyes.

The twenty-second letter of the Hebrew alphabet is Tav. It was originally portrayed in picture form as a cross. And while it represents a choice, it is the point where the beginning and end of a circle meet, or meet their ends. In modern times, mankind understands the Greek phrase "the Alpha and the Omega" as a name for God meaning "the Beginning and the End." The original Hebrew version of this verse is actually "the Aleph and the Tav," the first and last letters of the alphabet, the All and the Divine, the circle that is complete. But above all, the twenty-second letter is the choice one makes as to how the next part of His story shall be told.

Second Revelation

For me, the place I was most vulnerable was the Love held within my soul. In the first book I completed prior to this revelation, I explain how my soul had once been broken and shattered into a million pieces from my marriage that had ended before. It had taken me years to rebuild the framework of the man I once was, and ultimately would never again be. I was fragile, broken, and humbled before Him. The Love from within was my greatest point of vulnerability, for I knew that if I followed all that He willed and the lesson ended without the ending I desired, then my soul would undoubtedly shatter across the floor into an unrecognizable essence of someone that once was, and would never be forever more.

If there was one thing I could not give, it was the Love from pounding within my soul. But that is the test He used on me to gauge the strength of my Love for Him. Whether I was willing to follow every lead that he gave and place my soul in the ultimate place of vulnerability, that is everything – the complete package of my being – that I could possibly give to Him. In modern times, His test could only be done in this kind of way, for modern man must see a demonstration of faith in a way he can understand. If the same test of Abraham was to be rehashed in this generation, it would have to be in a way that no one would have expected to come. So as this second revelation is read, know that this was the leap of faith where I jumped, and He caught me in His hands.

...

Rebirth II

March 24, 2014
Late Evening

Yesterday I received a text from Lindsey thanking me for the gesture, but letting me know that she did not feel comfortable going to the bank or accepting the contents of the safety deposit box. As soon as I received that text, my heart sank. I cannot say I did not expect it at all – I still had high hopes that God would provide an improbable solution to the seemingly unraveling future with her. I held strong. Over the past few weeks I knew the day would come where I would see her with Chris.

It hurt. No doubt it hurt. But, as I sat there soaking it all in, I mustered up the only reply I could and told her I understood and asked her to return the key and book to a post office box I have for my company. Her text left me feeling like she was uncomfortable with everything I had written. That was not exactly the response I was looking for, but I have to believe an idea was planted. Yesterday, Lindsey had posted on twitter a quote saying something along the lines of "Sometimes we want God to provide for us, but only on our own time." It was interesting to see because it acknowledged that she understood Him reaching His hand out to her, but that she was resistant to the idea.

So after I replied back to her text, I sat on my couch in the darkness thinking about everything. I wrestled with the idea that either I was losing my mind, or that there was a pur-

Second Revelation

pose in what had happened. If anything, I felt more peace than any other feeling. I sat there numb to the surroundings just trying to digest it all. There were moments I felt sick to my stomach, and moments where I breathed a sigh of relief. All in all, I did not expect to feel the way I felt because the slew of emotions tossed around inside of me over the previous months had left me feeling rather helpless and broken at times. I could only expect this time I would be broken again. But I was not. Instead I was confused and introspective.

As I thought about how the book ended with her holding a key housed in clay and the remains of a bookmark that revealed a soul within, I searched for reason. Clearly God has been speaking to me this whole time. Clearly He has continued to show me undeniably amazing experiences in the heavens and with angels here on Earth. I actually started praying aloud for God to just turn off this messed up world and bring me up to heaven.

Let me underscore that it was not me asking for death, but rather for life. I wanted Him to just reveal everything because I no longer understood any part of it. My only options remaining in order to continue on during my earthly journey were: (1) to dismiss it all, suppress all that I thought I had been shown, and go back to just living life like all of the other oblivious people or (2) to accept the outcome as His will and continue onward on His path.

That was it. Those were the only two options. Nothing in between. This was a line drawn in the sand where I had to choose. Earlier in the day, God showed me I was a King. But I

Rebirth II

sat on my couch struggling with one single overarching concept that caused me to question everything: that concept was that I had no tangible proof of anything, which means it is all in my head.

I am probably one of the most analytical and reasonable people when it comes to unclouded and unbiased thought. So, as I sat on my couch in the darkness trying to rationalize everything I honestly found myself lost again. I could understand that the money spent on all of the arrangements for Lindsey's future was purposed into my life by God – so I could not be mad about spending it that way. I could understand all of the work He and the angels had shown me manifested in ways that would mount a defense that would withstand the toughest prosecutor. I would revisit the option of turning away from God, where it would seem that the only outcome was for a person to waste away on Earth.

Eventually I began to see that Lindsey – more importantly identified as the spiritual recognition of its counterpoint in another – was revealed a key to Ever-After, a life that would never have wants nor needs in any aspect. The overflowing demonstration of God providing an unquantifiable number of financial, emotional, and spiritual gifts for her future was apparent. Most importantly, the key was housed in clay. I began to see that this ever so important ending to the book that I was led to write, was intended for me to see and witness its significance. For if I were to continue on to the Promised Land, I would need to better understand the definition as the Kingdom of Eternal Love.

Second Revelation

To paraphrase the ending of the book, a soul was revealed the potential for a Love greater than it had ever known. The soul was shown that there was a key housed within the clay – symbolic to the body of the human – where all the person had to do was open the box. Instead, this soul chose to not open the box – to not even look inside. The only potential was greatness, and instead they feared what they saw. They feared the abundance being provided for them. In essence, the box contained a future of no wants and no worries for the rest of all time.

If I was to parallel this portion of my journey as a trial of being groomed as a King, this must be how God feels when He says to each person – "Here, I will offer you the Kingdom and everything within it. I will offer you perfection, Ever-After and a lifetime of beauty and Love. It is everything you thought you wanted and desired, plus much more. In fact, I will show you how to find it – how to find Me. There is a key within your body. All you have to do is use it. I will show you where the key is. I will tell you who I Am. I will even tell you what it unlocks and where to find it. The only action you have to take is to open the box."

It was then that I got it. I understood. Not only was it a parallel to all that God has offered through His words, through His message delivered through others in finding Him. But, it was a parallel to my earlier moment of Him showing me my seat as a King. On 3/24/2014, I was shown the Kingdom. This was the same day that Lindsey was shown the Kingdom on Earth – every spiritual truth manifested in a way for a per-

Rebirth II

fect life during her earthly walk. All she had to do was open the box. All I had to do was observe the dualities and choose to follow or return to before I was once saved. It was then as I thought about the dualities, that I also recognized again that Heaven and Earth are one. For, a person must see above as below, and the outer as the inner. I was witnessing everything in that moment as a testament to my walk. And as I thought about all that Lindsey was walking away from – all I could think about was how dumb it was not to open the box to see what was within.

With a blind arrogance and not even a desire to see, she chose the mundane over the ineffable. And in that, I knew I had no choice. My choice had been made long ago. I was not angry at her. In fact, I was heartbroken for her – not for me. It was the first time I have ever experienced this feeling, and it must be what spiritual Love feels like when it is lost. Because all I could feel was sadness for her – sadness that she did not even open the box. And while I thought about everything further, I realized that the ending I had written to the book that was intentionally left out of the ending to Lindsey's version of the book – the real ending which was sealed in an envelope that resided in the box she was to open – was only a potential of all that could be if she just sought to chase Love – and through that find God's ever-warming Love in His arms wrapped around her.

This was also the moment when I recognized how God must feel when someone turns away from Him. A person who has not been shown the key has somewhat of a larger playground to stumble and fall. Perhaps, God does not even judge them at all until they begin to see glimmers. And only then, when they have been shown the key, is a soul judged. This is all that is told in Deuteronomy 28. This is the verse I was given the day I signed my contract with Wilson. In this very moment, I was not witnessing my life fall apart – I was witnessing it fall together. This was the time that God said, "Here is the key. I've shown you the key. I've shown you everything I can to get you there. Now it is up to you to choose to use the key." And in that moment, I chose God. The day that God showed me the key and the day I chose to use it occurred on a day of His divine signs for me – 3/24/2014 – which adds to $3+2+4+2+0+1+4 = 16$, which totals $1+6 = 7$. Today was divine.

Requisition

May your faith through reading these words be found strong within. May you begin to see all that I began to see at this point as God's communication became more intimately bound. In the beginning, I approached the journey with science as my stallion. By the end of this portion of my journey, I had found an unbridled trust in my Father and the destination He was leading me unto. He asked me to leap, and I answered His call. And how more divinely planned than to test me through the bounds of Love? For He is Love and He wanted to show me that His Love was greater than All. For His Love is the Kingdom, the Father, The Foundation, Forever, and Evermore. Amen.

...
*From generations and generations to come,
this is the revelation of His Love Divine.*
...

www.ingramcontent.com/pod-product-compliance
Lightning Source LLC
Chambersburg PA
CBHW021140080526
44588CB00008B/142